Didaskalos Books

THE FIFTH CANDLE OF ADVENT

José Granados

THE FIFTH CANDLE OF ADVENT

Meditations for each day

didaskalos

Nihil obstat:
Fr. Gary Selin
Imprimatur:
The Most Rev. Samuel J. Aquila
Archbishop of Denver, Colorado
November 10, 2012, Feast of St. Leo the Great

Originally published in Spanish as *La quinta vela del Adviento*, Ciudad Nueva, Madrid 2007. English translation copyright © 2012 by Disciples of the Hearts of Jesus and Mary Inc., Littleton, CO.

Excerpts from the *Lectionary for Mass for Use in the Dioceses of the United States of America, second typical edition* © 2001, 1998, 1997, 1986, 1970 Confraternity of Christian Doctrine, Inc., Washington, DC. Used with permission. All rights reserved. No portion of this text may be reproduced by any means without permission in writing from the copyright owner.

Cover design by Enrique Sotomayor – Virginia Wollstein
Photograph by Karyn Byrne

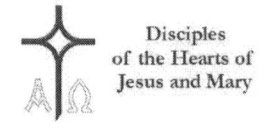

Disciples of the Hearts of Jesus and Mary

The Disciples of the Hearts of Jesus and Mary want to express our debt of gratitude to Caroline Chihoski, Janet Watson and the "Friends of the Disciples" who have helped us to make a reality this book, offering with unbounded generosity their time, talent and treasure.
God bless you.

Copyright © 2012, José Granados - Didaskalos Books, Littleton, CO
All rights reserved
ISBN: 978-0-61571-905-4
ISBN: 0-61571-905-8
Printed in the United States of America

To my father, sower of advents

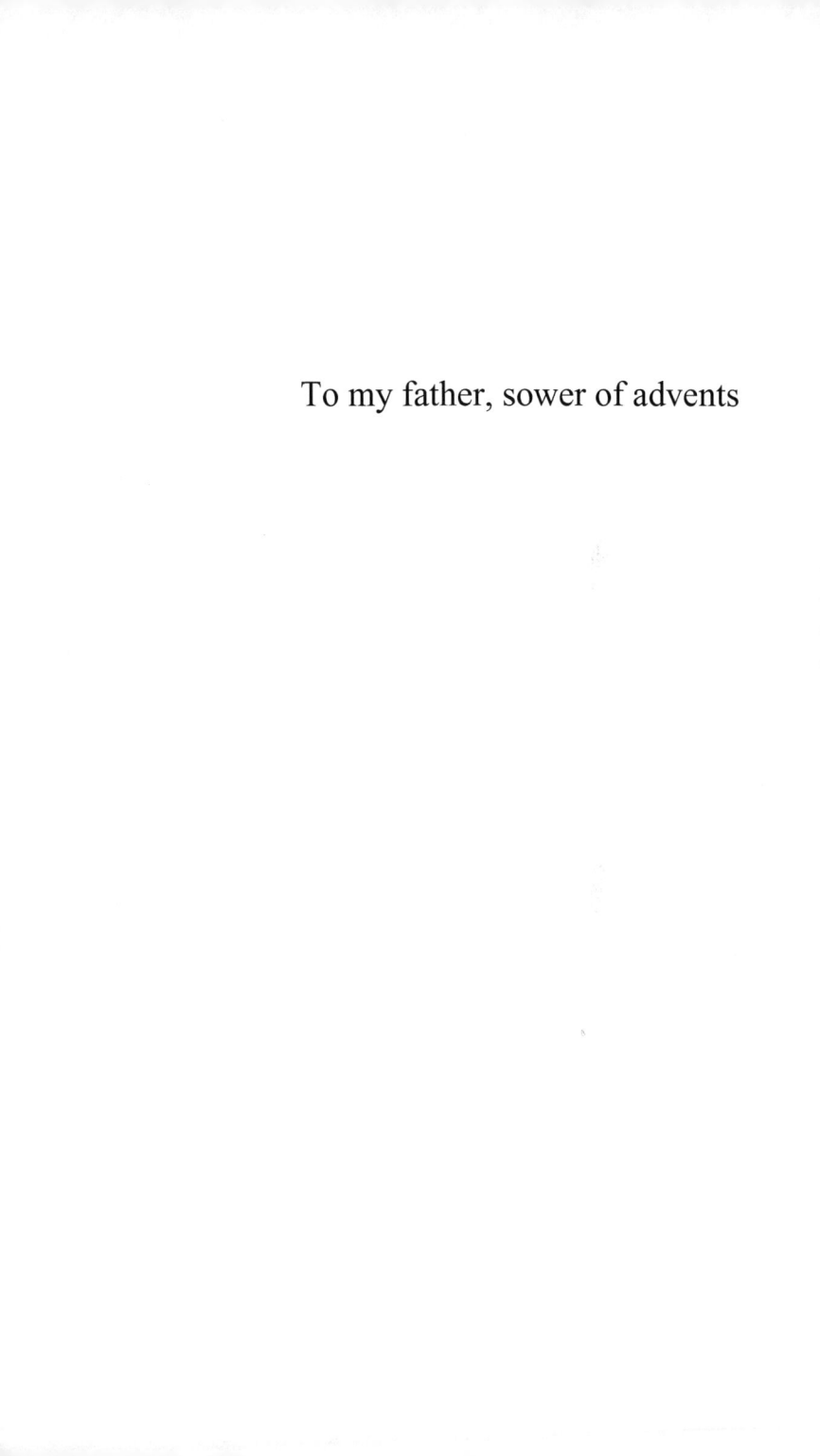

Contents

Introduction		9

FIRST WEEK

Sunday A:	Awakening our Desire	15
Sunday B:	The Final Christmas	19
Sunday C:	Opening New Paths	22
Monday:	The Comings and Goings of Advent	25
Tuesday:	The Peace of the Children	28
Wednesday:	Toward the Stars	32
Thursday:	The Rock of Hope	35
Friday:	The Eyes of Hope	38
Saturday:	The End has Become the Path	42

SECOND WEEK

Sunday A:	The Spirit Who Overtakes Us	45
Sunday B:	Traveled Paths	50
Sunday C:	Learn to Return	53
Monday:	A Holy Way	56
Tuesday:	Joy, the Food for our Journey	58
Wednesday:	The Starred Circle	61
Thursday:	Making Oneself Small	64
Friday:	Cold or Heat at Christmas	67
Saturday:	The Hope of Creation	70

THIRD WEEK

Sunday A:	The Joys of the Sad One	75
Sunday B:	The Joy of the One Who Waits	81
Sunday C:	The Joy of Pilgrims	84
Monday:	Seeing From Afar	87
Tuesday:	A Road for the Few	90
Wednesday:	Hope in the Shoot and Hope in the Fruit	93
Thursday:	A Return Path	96
Friday:	The Baptist in Advent	98

FOURTH WEEK

Sunday A:	The Path After the Path	103
Sunday B:	The House of God is Your House	107
Sunday C:	Encounter From the Mother's Womb	111

WEEKDAYS OF ADVENT AFTER DECEMBER 17

December 17: He Assumed in Him the Ancient	117
December 18: Joseph, Paternity and the Future	121
December 19: The Priest in a Diaper	125
December 20: The Sign of the Virgin	129
December 21: May My Eyes Behold You	132
December 22: To Return Love Back	135
December 23: Giving Tomorrow a Name	138
December 24: Awaken, Oh Man!	141
Christmas: Christmas: Recognizing our Origins	143

SPECIAL FEASTS

November 20: St. Andrew: Missionary Advent	151
December 8: The Immaculate: a Taste of Christmas	154

Introduction

It is well known that the Advent wreath has four candles, nearly always purple in color. We light them one by one at the Mass on Sunday as Christmas approaches. In our family, we used to light them every afternoon during Advent when our parents would gather us to pray for a while in preparation for the birth of Jesus. We sat around a mystery with St. Joseph and the Virgin, the mule and the ox; only the Child was missing because our mother would hide it in a drawer in the dining room. She would later take Him out in procession, amid carols on Christmas Eve. We would share a brief prayer and count the days until Christmas.

The candles were our path, our steps, through the cold nights of Advent. The purple signified our effort to arrive at the Crèche with the other shepherds and drummer boys. I remember that near the crown of candles there always was a jar where each one would secretly place a bean during the day. A bean was placed for each small sacrifice offered to the child Jesus in preparation for his arrival. Later I read that Mother Teresa of Calcutta did something similar, but instead of beans she used straw that would later be used to line the manger for the Child. Undoubtedly the manger would be much softer with straw rather than beans.

Introduction

Advent is a time for joyous effort and for joyful tension. Other moments of conversion, like Lent, can be represented by a road through the desert, under a burning sun, carrying a heavy load for our sins. Not so Advent; Advent is rather a night route in which the Pilgrim walks lightly with wings of hope, feeling the light night air on his face.

Of course, the path of Advent is not easy either; although it is not taken with the burden of the desert, one must carry another burden, that of darkness. The pain of Advent, the pile of beans accumulated day by day, takes this form: that of not knowing what is coming around the bend, walking by feel, in small steps. It requires a special activity from us, that we maintain the desire for the light so that we will not fall asleep when tired of waiting.

The candles of Advent remind us that it is time to put before God the shadows that inhabit our life: the project that we have begun without knowing how it will end; the bumps we are hitting in our relationship with someone in our family or with a co-worker; the mess we have gotten into and from which we cannot extricate ourselves; the development of an illness that worries us...All of us carry a handful of unknowns in our sack; being able to take them in hand is the gift and the task of Advent.

And so, the candles of our Advent wreath measure the stages of this liturgical time. They remind us that our steps toward Christmas are not measured by the length of our stride, but by the time that remains until the day arrives. It is not as essential for those who walk in darkness to advance their steps as it is to follow the course of the stars and the Hope that light will be growing up.

Consequently, the four candles will always be incomplete. On the horizon of Advent, the hope of a fifth candle remains. It is the candle that human effort can never light, and the only candle able to light our night like the dawn disperses our darkness. This candle must be lit by God, and he uses the wax that he has generously put in our wreath, lighting in it a new luminosity.

Therefore, the great mystery of Advent is not our path, but the path of God toward us. It is time to discover that the Christian God is a God that comes. He is always coming to meet us; he is a God whose most intimate knowledge is that of knowing how to come nearer to us. He is a traveling God, a God that comes and tears the heavens to light the night.

In our journey of Advent, we prepare to recognize that candle, the fifth in the crown, which will shine on Christmas day. Its brilliance will fill us with wonder because of its smallness.

On the path of life we look several times for a light to solve everything, and to show us a complete vision of the path we must travel, like lightning allows us, for a moment, to glimpse an entire valley across the darkness. This Advent let us accustom our sight to a different kind of light. The light of God, brighter than at noon, will

Introduction

always be a humble light; a light that the Mother will protect in Bethlehem—in the way that hands protect the flame of a candle, worried that the wind will extinguish it. This light, made small, can then enter our homes and light them from within: the light of love lights thus.

These meditations are meant to help us recognize the light of that fifth candle and to keep our eyes open to receive it. One can follow the rhythm of the liturgical days by the brief prayer of each day of our journey. Keep in mind the two stages of Advent: until the third Sunday we follow the days of the week, from Monday to Saturday; then on December 17 begins the countdown until December 24, and each day has its proper reading. At the end of the book, we have included some feasts that always or nearly always occur during Advent; St. Andrew (November 30) and the Feast of the Immaculate Conception (December 8). This book also lends itself to be read straight ahead without following the liturgical rhythm. When read straight through, we desire this book to be a path of hope. When read while following the steps of Advent, it lights the wreath while awaiting the mysterious light, blinding in its humility, of that fifth candle.

First Week

Sunday Year A

Awakening our Desire

"It is the hour now for you to awake from sleep...put on the LORD Jesus Christ" (Rom 13:11.14)

"So too, you also must be prepared, for at an hour you do not expect, the Son of Man will come" (Mt 24:44)

On the first Sunday in Advent when the lector approaches to proclaim the epistle, he will read the Bible at the same place where St. Augustine, a long time ago, opened it during a very crucial moment in his life.

The saint was battling against himself. He wanted to surrender to God, but at the same time he realized his insufficient strength; he was too attached to his bad habits. Then he heard the voice of a child singing in the adjacent garden, "Take and read, take and read..." Nearby there happened to be a manuscript with the letters of St. Paul. Upon opening it, Augustine read the same text we see today, which starts our Advent season, "not in orgies and drunkenness, not in promiscuity and licentiousness...Put on the Lord Jesus Christ" (Rom 13:13-14; Confessions VIII, 12:29).

"What do you desire, Augustine?" God asked him at that crucial moment. And it is the same question he asks us as we begin our Advent journey. What do you desire? Can you examine the desires that are in your heart in the same manner that you examine your conscience to determine your sins? This examination is necessary because our desires are the impulse that pushes us to walk.

What happened to St. Augustine was that his desires were sickly, as though his wings were atrophied and had converted into chains that impeded flight. Later the saint would describe the situation in the same way that Jesus does in today's Gospel: our desires are asleep (cf. Mt 24:42-43). It is similar to the feeling a person has when he must arise, but he wishes to continue sleeping. He realizes that he must be awake because that is the true life, where one is constructive and productive; however, he chooses to coil up in his dreams.

The same happens to us. We wish to enjoy the affection and consolation of others: of our husband or wife, of our children, parents, and siblings. But many times we do not make out, in the heart of that desire, the call to build a lasting friendship, and to get out of ourselves and help others grow. Our love just stays as the fireworks of the sentiment. It is incapable on its own of opening a path to greater horizons. We can say then that our desires are dormant. What differentiates sleep from vigilance is that in sleep we cannot walk; in sleep all ends in the evanescent instant. It is like in nightmares where we run and never reach our goal. Or it is like other dreams in which everything is repetitive, and it is impossible to escape a thousand perils.

Sunday Year A

When we start Advent, it is time to awaken, and to learn to desire what will help us to grow. How can we achieve this? We must introduce what will make our desires great and true, capable of maturing without atrophy. In all of the desires that motivate your life—the desire to have a happy family life, to prosper in your work, to give your children a good future—beat a great, hidden desire that allows you to have expectations beyond your limitations, despite the threats of an uncertain tomorrow. It is the desire for God himself. He is the only one who can fill your heart and teach you to truly love your brothers. Discover that desire in the depths of your desires. Make it shine again with a strong light. It will give vigor to all you await and fill you with what your heart longs for.

We understand then the need for prayer during Advent: he who prays learns to desire God and learns to enlarge his desires so that the Lord will fit within them. In that sense Benedict XVI has spoken of prayer as the language of hope (cf. *Spe Salvi* 32-34). To pray is to take your life in your hands as someone who nears a dormant fire and blows patiently to rekindle the embers of that desire for God: a living fire will then illuminate from within every daily care that engulfs you.

Augustine awoke when he read the text from St. Paul, which we read today. It was a great voice that took him out of his lethargy; it was the powerful calling of the Lord Jesus, "put on the Lord Jesus Christ." The ultimate secret of our human desires is then revealed to us: only a great love can awaken us, transform our desires, and start us on our journey. Only because God loved us first (cf. 1 Jn 4:19) are we able to start looking for him. We can learn to desire God because we know that he wishes to be with mankind, and that he wishes it so strongly that he is readying himself to travel toward our home, toward Bethlehem, toward our Christmas...

Sunday Year B

The Final Christmas

"Be watchful! Be alert! You do not know when the time will come" (Mk 13:33)
"Grace to you and peace from God our Father and the LORD Jesus Christ" (1 Cor 1:3)

The text in which St. Bernard distinguishes three comings of the Lord is well known (cf. *5th Sermon on Advent*). One coming is in the past, when he was born in Bethlehem; another is in the present, when he comes to be received in the Eucharist; and a third is in the future, when he will visit us at the end of time. We tend to remember with joy of the first coming and to await with delight the daily coming during the Mass. But that last coming, on the terrible and glorious day of judgment, rather causes us fear. Who desires the end of the world? Wouldn't it be better that we ask God to give us some more time, delay the end, and not hurry his arrival?

However the first Christians prayed that the Lord would hurry, and that he would not delay. "*Maranatha!*" meaning "Come Lord Jesus," (cf. 1 Cor 16:22; Rv 22:20) was a prayer that asked for his glorious return. The hosanna that we pray in the Eucharist had the same meaning in the old days, "Blessed he who comes to rule forever, to bring the justice and peace that never end!" Should we not hold the same desire in our lives that he would come? If we await Christmas joyfully, shouldn't we be joyful at the last Christmas of God, when he will be born from within all things?

It is important that we perceive with clarity our fear of the final coming of Jesus, since it reveals the truth of our hearts. Our fear teaches us that we do not desire that the Lord come today to transform our lives. If you say you love the first rays of dawn, should you not also yearn for the bright sunlight of noon? In the same way, those who yearn for the Lord's presence today, would they not also anxiously await his last coming? If we fear our last encounter with him, maybe we do not desire to meet him today either. Maybe we fear what his love may demand of us and the transformation that encountering the living God will cause in us?

It is important to truly desire the last coming of Christ, if we wish to cultivate the vigilance that Jesus asks of us in the Gospel (cf. Mk 13:33). It is true that our fear of the last day surprising us, with our hands empty, will encourage us to be alert. But that fear in itself is not strong enough to force our eyes to remain alert. Only love, the desire that the day arrive, will have true vigilance as its fruit. Now then, is it possible to enliven that desire? Can we do it without abandoning the world and all we love in it? The readings for today give us a clue as to the answers to those questions.

The first is taken from the last chapters of the book of Isaiah (cf. Is 63-64). Israel is suffering in exile for its sins and goes to God—as though it needs to remind him, in case he has forgotten, of the love he has for his people. It is one of the few times in the Old Testament when God is called Father. "LORD, you are our father, /we are the clay and you are the potter; /we are all the work of your hand" (Is 64:7). St. Paul already sees the fulfillment of the promise and wishes for the Corinthians "the grace and peace from God our Father" whom he dares to call "my God" because of his extreme closeness, and he says that God is faithful and has called us to be companions of his Son (cf. 1 Cor 1:3-9).

This is the secret for not being fearful of the last coming: God is our father. We come from him; in him we have our true home, and before him we are truly ourselves. That means that separated from him we can do nothing; we have nothing; we are nothing. To desire his coming is to learn to receive all from him so that we may know the true life. St. Augustine exhorted Christians, fearful of the last coming of Christ, to follow him now as a shepherd so that you may not fear him when he comes as judge. We can add: accept him now as father to truly wish his final coming, in which he will give us birth again, and definitely.

The Church, with its liturgy, wishes that we unite our wait for the final coming with the wait for Christmas, for the birth of Jesus. And if the final judgment is the final Christmas, why should we be afraid? Is anybody afraid of the birth of a son?

First week

Opening New Paths

"To you, O LORD, I lift my soul" (Ps 25:1)
"Stand erect and raise your heads" (Lk 21:28)

In life there are many ways to find a path. For example, those who follow a wounded animal have to walk slowly, looking with care at the ground so as not to miss the slightest detail. A crushed blade of grass or a smudged paw print in the mud can reveal that the prey has passed by that place. This is why the tracker walks bowed down, noticing where he should put his feet.

That technique is not useful in all our searches. What happens when we have to open new paths, and travel where no one has gone before?

It is necessary, for example, to break a vice in which you fall continuously; or you may need to forgive a person with whom you have had enmity for a long time; or perhaps you must make a difficult decision that will change your life; maybe your children are growing older, and you have to discover how to continue educating them; or you realize that your relationship with your husband or wife is entering a new stage that requires different ways to express your love…

Opening new paths. That is precisely the message of Advent, which we embark on today. It invites you to break the old routes and take a new one; one that will take you further from your old self. The path of Advent thus cannot be taken by someone who insists on continuing bent down, looking at the ground. What different way is offered to us?

We must watch another one who looks for paths, the navigator. He also has to find routes that will take him to port. But, unlike the tracker, he cannot look down because he will not find more clues than the fleeting froth. If his path is always a new one through the waves, where will the sailor look? The answer is he looks on high to the skies. There he sees the star that indicates the path he is to take to make it through the night.

And that is, in effect, what today's readings tell us. In the Psalm we pray, "To you, O Lord, I lift my soul" (Ps 25:1). And in the Gospel, Jesus encourages us, "Stand erect and raise your heads" (Lk 21: 28), so that we can "stand before the Son of Man" (Lk 21:36).

The one who looks only to the earth will never find a new way. He will go in circles, around himself. His love will consist of routine and boredom. To the one who wishes to start a new path, there is only one solution: to look upward. The new path always comes from above, from God. Do you want to forgive and have never done it before? Look up, see the way that God loves and forgives you. Do you want the love of your family to grow without falling into a routine expression? Look up and find out that your brothers are a gift from the Father. Put God in the center of your love so that he will make it inexhaustible. Where there is no path to follow, the North Star alone can show the way.

Advent trains us to look toward God. The poet said, "Tie your plow to a star" The plow, an instrument that moves in our daily plantings, can be tied to a star of high paths, and precisely so, will make our furrows deep and fertile. The juicy fruits that surprise us by their novelty can only come from heaven. We will celebrate it on Christmas Eve; the day when we will receive the child Jesus, the symbol of gift and surprise. "Behold, I make all things new" (Rev 21:5).

Monday

The Comings and Goings of Advent

"Come, let us climb the LORD's mountain" (Is 2:3)
"I will come and cure him (Mt 8:7)
"Many will come from the east and the west, and will recline…at the banquet" (Mt 8:11)

Advent is a time of journey and a time of being on the go. The birth of a child is announced, and there is a great agitation. In our soul something stirs as well, awakening the desire to prepare new ways. In the history of the centurion, which the Gospel relates today (cf Mt 8:5-11), the comings and goings of this season are condensed and presage the coming of Christmas.

The centurion goes to Jesus to plead, "Lord my servant is lying and home." In Advent, in the first place, our misery is on the move. It is a time for poverty, because only truly felt poverty—felt in our own flesh—permits the hope of health. From the abyss of our weakness a true prayer rises to God.

And we say "Lord, I am not worthy that to should enter under my roof." These are the words we repeat before receiving each Eucharist, the daily coming of the Lord. The Church repeats them now in preparation for the mystery of Christmas. Lord, the world is not worthy that you come to dwell in it. Look well at what you do and where you are descending to.

"I will come and cure him." God ignores our objection and comes to our house. In Advent we all march to prepare for a birth; however, the first one to start out is the Son of God. "Your word descended in the midst of silence," we will say on Christmas Eve. On Christmas, the Son of God will make himself "sharer in our pains to heal them" (St. Justin, Apologia II:13); an odd physician who wishes to suffer with his patients to administer medicine. "I will come and cure him."

There are still more people on the road, "Many will come from the East and the West and recline at the banquet in the kingdom of Heaven." Because you have confessed your unworthiness—Jesus seems to say to the Centurion—not only will I come to your house but you will enter into my house and you will recline with me at my table. Thus Advent refers us to the ultimate finish. It refers us to the time when we will unite with all peoples in the house of the Father. God comes to us to bring us to himself, and to his own dwelling place. Then we understand that maybe the fundamental questions of life are not, "where do we come from?" or "where are we going?" but instead "who is coming to us?" and "where are we being taken?"

That is the road of Advent. Not only are we on the road, God is also on the road. We go to encounter someone who is coming—who is already preparing the suitcases and buying the tickets. For our part, we laze about; we waste the days of grace. God, however, is

Monday

diligent and on the first Monday is living intensely his Advent, and is nearing us. To know that he is on the way helps us to take the first steps. "Come let us climb the LORD's mountain, /to the house of the God of Jacob" (Is 2:3).

First week

The Peace of the Children

"The calf and the young lion shall browse together" (Is 11:6)
"You have hidden these things from the wise and the learned" (Lk 10:21)

The first reading presents to us an idyllic vision: the calf and the lion feeding together. It is an image of the peace that the Messiah will bring. Peace that will exist even between peoples that have lived in hate since time immemorial. It can seem unattainable to us, like a tale meant to deceive the unwary. And we become more skeptical as the years pass. We realize that many men are wolves to other men, and we feel that it is pretty difficult for them to change.

We need then to read today's Gospel and see how Jesus gives thanks because God has revealed these things to the humble and simple and hidden them from the wise and powerful. In that way we understand something very important on our path in Advent. Only the small, those who have the eyes of a child, can expect a miracle of peace as great as the one promised by the prophet. Only those who know they are children can believe that Christmas is possible even in the midst of the daily difficulties.

What gives the child that power? To understand we must reflect on what causes war. The primordial violence comes from an interior battle. It stems from an internal division against our very selves. Secretly we don't accept our own lives or our situations in the world. We reject our personal history. We rebel against our very existence because of our unfulfilled plans, our frustrated desires. And from our hearts rise irritation, impatience, and resentment. Confronted with our own lives, it is not strange that we become irritable with others and discord grows amid brothers.

On the other hand, the one that recognizes that the root of his existence and the secret of his personality are in being a child, and in laying on another the secret of his own life, is then capable of looking at himself and at the world in a new way. The child has peace because he accepts that his origins are from another; he knows that his beginnings are from another and that the other is the good father, the Creator. Such a person can then accept his history as it is. He can accept himself in his life, work, suffering, and love. Even his faults, which he knows are forgiven, turn out to be a reminder of mercy and a fountain of joy. That person sees the path to original harmony as continually open to a place where all is well. He discovers in the midst of the heart of things a first kindness more primitive than the fault that stains those things, and so he is able to confront them.

And so, the one who accepts himself as a child discovers that radical kindness also in the brother that has offended him. He knows that, beyond the actions he observes, within each person there is a never-ending spring of regeneration. It is a spring that comes from our common Father. From this grateful gaze at our own life, we learn to look at our brothers in another fashion and to accept their presence and concrete history as a gift from God. Which leads us to say: pardon is possible because you are greater than the evil committed, because in you there is no limit to hope, and because God loves you and has entrusted you to my care. And so, founded in God, from whom hopes all things, love expects all from our brother (cf. 1 Cor 13:7).

Saint Bernard distinguished between various types of people of peace. There is on the one part, the one that enjoys tranquility and has no problems, the *homo pacatus* (the pacified man). It is a level of peace that is very unstable because it depends solely on external circumstances. As soon as the wind stirs up a bit and anxiety rises, the peace will disappear. Instead we must continue to grow in peace, and one must make oneself *homo pacificus* (peaceful man). The peaceful man is he who keeps peaceful in the midst of attacks from the enemy. He carries peace internally, not only externally. Therefore the key to the fountain of peace is to accept oneself as a child: then one enjoys the peace of the

Tuesday

beginning, which is based on the good gaze of the God that blessed creation.

Some doubts surface as we consider these thoughts. Is this all the fruit of ingenuity? Don't we have proof that reconciliation is impossible? We must then look at Jesus, prince of peace, born on the night of peace. For it to be possible for a *homo pacificus* to exist, we need the *homo pacificans*, the one that makes us peaceful. That is Christ, who is able to create peace around himself, and is able to bring back hope in the radical kindness of the world. Because he is the Son who has come to accept all his life as a gift from the Father: all that he has and is, and all that he enjoys and suffers. If the lamb and the lion will browse together it is because there is "a little child to guide them" (Is 11:6).

First week

Toward the Stars

> "The LORD of hosts/ will provide.../A feast of rich food" (Is 25:6)
> "They picked up the fragments left over –seven baskets full" (Mt 15:37)

The first week of Advent makes us look toward the last Advent, which is the glorious Parousia of the Lord. The readings today uncover for us what the last coming of Christ will be like. Isaiah says that the Lord God will provide for all peoples, on this mountain, a succulent feast (cf. Is 25:6). And in the Gospel we read the multiplication of the loaves (cf. Mt 15:29-37).

The coming of the Lord is compared thus with complete satiety. Advent is then the moment to feel hunger, and to become aware of the depths of our desires that only God can satisfy.

The great Italian poet Dante Alighieri knew well the desires of the human heart. In the three parts of his *Divine Comedy* "Hell," "Purgatory," and "Paradise," he tells the path of humanity, detached from God by sin, until he arrives and sees his Creator. It is known that the three parts of the poem end with the same word "stars." When he left hell, Dante said that he again "could see the stars." Upon escaping purgatory, he is "disposed to rise to the stars." When he reaches the heights of heaven and the

Wednesday

vision of God, he says he was in ecstasy looking "at the love that moves the sun and the others stars." The poet wished to express that looking up to the stars in the heavens is the only way to know who we are, and the only way to find our road. Hell is the place where the stars cannot be seen because hope has been abandoned there. What man desires is to always climb to the stars—an effort that is superior to his ability.

It is not bad, sometimes, to feel the sadness of not being able to reach those stars. The one who occasionally feels poor and sad can feel the desire to look up. Wherever we may be, whether things are going well or not, whether our spirits are down or we feel like we are on the cloud nine, we must always leave a hole in our heart for God to fill.

Let us remember what is told of Alexander the Great. When his soldiers sacked with avarice the gold of a rich city recently conquered he remained immutable astride his horse. "Don't you want anything?" one of his generals asked. The reply was "I prefer to just stay with my hope." Let us then leave a hole for hope. Do we want to know how the last day, that final Parousia that we recall in the first week of Advent, will be? Let us notice how large is our nostalgia for the presence and gift of God.

The Gospel today tells us that after satiating the hunger of the multitude, Jesus had many leftover baskets full of bread. God always has a surprise up his sleeve; his heights are greater than our depths; his joy is larger than our nostalgia. The theologian Joseph Ratzinger said in his *Introduction to Christianity* that one of the fundamental laws of being Christian is the law of excess: there is in the Gospel a superabundance, an exaggeration of love and giving that is greater than any expectation.

That is why Advent means being ready to learn and to receive something new from God. Dante, upon reaching heaven, contemplated what was greater than the stars and above the expectations of human beings, because it was what makes all things happen: the love of God, "the love that moves the sun and the rest of the stars." This is what Jesus distributed while he was on earth, what he gives us in the daily Eucharist, and what he will give us on the last day's feast.

Thursday

The Rock of Hope

"A strong city have we... /the LORD is an eternal Rock" (Is 26:1,4)

"A wise man who built his house on rock...." (Mt 7:24)

In today's reading, the prophet Isaiah describes a strong city in which dwells a faithful nation, walled, with firm foundations. In that way, at the beginning of Advent we are invited to meditate on the foundation of our hope. The one who has hope trusts that his future will be good. He can view the future with a calm gaze. Many times, however, we confuse hope with optimism. And yet there is a great difference between them.

How are they different? While optimism is a vague state or disposition toward life, the one who has hope has total security about his future. We can say that hope has a foundation; it is not a castle in the air or on sand. Hope is like a city that can raise high walls and offer security to its inhabitants against the inclemency of the weather or the attack of enemies—precisely because it is well founded and because it is based on the rock.

Again we ask ourselves if that is possible, and if one can be certain about the future. Our response: in hope, the future is already present and offers us solid proof that it will arrive. That means that hope is not only about what will happen tomorrow. It is based on something great that has already happened and transformed our lives. It is based on a present possession that is rock solid and allows us to build up high.

That rock, that foundation is love. Is it not true that when love appears in our life, we discover in it the promise of happiness; that is to say, an advance on tomorrow? That is the promise that made us take the path of matrimony, receive with joy our children, and renew the course of a broken friendship—Because we had seen in that love something that made us have confidence in the future, and that offered us foundations on which to build.

However, all loves ultimately show fragility: they are not sufficiently strong to carry the weight of a life or the battles of all the uncertainties of life. Only the love of God can be the true rock that permits us to raise an entire city. Those who build on him will not be defrauded. We are reminded by Isaiah to "Trust in the Lord forever, for the Lord is an eternal Rock." So that love has revealed itself as totally faithful. It is faithful to the point of coming us at Christmas to sign an irrevocable alliance. That is why Christian hope is also compared to an anchor (cf. Heb 6:19). Let us notice that it isn't the kind of anchor that attaches a boat to the bottom of the sea; it is the one that the mountain climber throws upward to attach to the rock and help him in climbing the mountain.

In the Gospel, Jesus explains the true foundation of our salvation, the solid hope, is not our words "Lord,

Lord" (cf Mt 7:21). What sustains us are the words of God in which he reveals his will; words that we possess when we listen and follow them. The one who has discovered the love of God and has allowed it to transform his life and already has a promise that converts into the foundation of a firm hope: the hope that does not defraud because it is built on a love that has covered the cost ahead of time.

First week

The Eyes of Hope

"On that day... out of gloom and darkness the eyes of the blind shall see" (Is 29:18)
"And their eyes were opened" (Mt 9:30)

The longest nights of the year happen during Advent. As the days advance, they become darker and yet, our hope of a great light grows, urging us to light a new candle each week. We will light four, one each Sunday, and we will await the Lord himself to light the fifth, that of his coming to Bethlehem. So today, the Gospel reminds us of the importance of light when two blind men beg that the Lord will "Have pity on us," and Jesus heals them.

We might ask for the light that Jesus brings while we wait. What is the light of Advent like? In effect there are different lights—one for each of the dark moments that we traverse. However, the darkness of the Advent night is the distinctive darkness of future. We do not know what tomorrow will bring and that can cause anxiety and fear. In the military there are infrared glasses that permit people to see in the dark. Do we have similar glasses that will allow us to see the future?

The first light to illuminate our future is the light of our desire. St. Augustine explains it thus: imagine that you forget the name of someone you know. Several

Friday

possibilities come to mind. Was his name Anthony, Peter, James? One by one we discard with certainty each one as the name does not fit with the face. St. Augustine concludes that in some way you have to know the name of that person, even though you do not fully remember the name. Otherwise, how could you be sure that the name is neither Anthony, nor Peter, nor James, even if you do not know yet that his name is John?

The same thing occurs with our search for happiness. We are attracted to many desires, hoping to find fulfillment. We think that what moves us and give us happiness is to succeed in our work, our vacations that come, or that a tough period will pass...But later, when the moment we awaited arrives, we realize that it has not brought us happiness. And we say "No, that wasn't it." St. Augustine asks us: how can you be sure that is not it if you don't in some way know what you are looking for? There has to be in you, in the center of your being, your heart of hearts, a memory of what you are yearning for. God must have touched you, must have wounded you with a sore that will long forever for the only antidote that can heal it—that is the very presence of God and communion with Him. This is the light of desire and the thirst that illuminates at night and permits us to search for the source.

But that light of desire is still very small. It cannot light much. It only urges us to continue to look forward and reminds us at each step that we have not yet arrived

First week

at the end. Is there a more powerful light that will help us to sort out our steps?

That light does exist; it is the light of hope. If we have spoken in the Christian tradition of the eyes of faith and also the eyes of charity, there are also the eyes of hope, eyes made to see what is to come. We can compare this to what happens when a friend promises us something. We trust in our friend. We know that he is faithful and will get done what he promised. In that way, the future, which was all darkness, starts to clear up. We have a sure point that will orient us: whatever happens, there is one thing that will not change—something will happen without a doubt, because our friend will be faithful. Confident of that promise, we receive at once the certain light of what will come in our future.

That is what happens to the two blind men. Jesus asks, "Do you believe that I can do this, that I can give you your sight?" Their faith in Jesus, their confidence in his power to give them their sight, allows them to regain their eyesight. The Christian hope springs when Jesus himself promises us that he will quench the thirst of our desire. Jesus is already our friend, and he has everything we can wait for. Your future goes through him; you must find it in him. His steps on earth indicate where you must set your steps. They are the path that will guide you beyond the anxiety of your future. You know that, regardless of how things change, there will always be a firm rock, a safe place, a hand extended permanently toward you. That is why as soon as the blind men opened their eyes, they saw the face of Jesus. That was all they needed to illuminate their way.

When we walk in the dark this Advent, when we feel the weight of uncertainty, when many projects of our life are doubtful, and when the outcomes of our hopes are dimming or already dashed...let us stop a while and ask God for his light, the light of hope. Maybe with it we can only see the next small steps that we need to make. It may seem that it does not enlighten much. But the light of hope is in reality very powerful. Like that of the distant stars, it permits us to find north and then go on our way for the remainder of the night or even thousand nights that we must still travel. The light of hope makes us realize that we have as fellow traveler the fountain of light himself.

First week

The End has Become the Path

"This is the way, walk in it" (Is 30:21)
"At the sight of the crowds, his heart was moved with pity for them" (Mt 9:36)

The prophet Isaiah tells us today, "No longer will your Teacher hide himself, /but with your own eyes you shall see your Teacher, /While from behind, a voice shall sound in your ears: /This is the way; walk in it." Man is accustomed to getting near to God by signs and images, kind of making some detours; he is used to having God hidden and to having him silent. Well then, the prophet says there will be a day when that will no longer occur. It will not be necessary to go round and round to find God and to understand his will because we will hear his voice behind us saying, "This is the way."

How will that happen? The prophet did not give us an explanation. We know it because we await Christmas. We realize the marvel of the words of Isaiah, "With your own eyes you will see your Teacher." Who would have suspected such closeness? We will contemplate him in the cradle at Bethlehem.

And yet we know that many times the will of God does not appear with the clarity that we desire. Do we have the impression that God is still hiding? What has changed? Where is the voice that says to us, "This is the way, walk in it?"

The one who looks at Jesus receives the response. Rather than tell us each step of the way that we must travel through life, God has given us a living way (cf. Heb 10:20) that goes before us. He tells us, "This is the way," when he walks before us and bids us to follow him.

We can now pay attention to the Gospel. Jesus was moved with pity at the sight of the crowds. It is true that Isaiah had described the way a person should approach God; he had told us that we could see and hear him. But he had not explained that from the point of view of God himself. If he had, he would not only have said, "That day you shall see your Teacher," but also, "That day the Heart of the Teacher will be moved with pity for you."

If we look at this from the point of view of God, Advent is a way of compassion. In the words of St. Bernard, quoted by Benedict XVI in his encyclical *Spe Salvi*, "God cannot suffer, but he can suffer with" (*Spe Salvi* 39). And he who is moved with pity, moves and gets near to where love takes him.

"Without cost you have received, without cost you are to give" concludes the Gospel. As God makes his way toward us, our Advent journey must also come into contact with the problems and miseries of our brothers and sisters. We cannot stay away from them, loving them at a distance. Advent is path toward his poverty, "to bind up the wounds" and "heal the bruises left by his blows."

First week

May the God of compassion teach us to be compassionate, to move toward the others, to heal the pain of others, and so to make ourselves, like Jesus, a new and living way for our brothers.

Second Week

Sunday Year A

The Spirit Who Overtakes Us

"The Spirit of the LORD shall rest upon him" (Is 11:2)
"He will baptize you with the Holy Spirit and fire" (Mt 3:11)

We encounter John the Baptist at the beginning of Lent and again now, at the beginning of Advent. That is because all Christian conversion, every preparation of our soul for the arrival of God, needs to have first the figure of the precursor. What special message does John the Baptist have for this season of the year?

John directs us now to our concrete situation of poverty and sin. We see that in our life justice, peace, and forgiveness are missing. We live in enmity with each other; like the wolf and the lamb, like the serpent and the dove. It seems that we do not move while Christmas nears, and it will surprise us in a state of unreadiness, without getting ready a room for Jesus at the inn.

John brings to our misery the balm of the Spirit. As Isaiah says in the first reading, the spirit of the Lord will descend in all its fullness to reestablish the peace that existed at the beginning of the world, when there were no enemies or violence.

Who is this Spirit? Because of Christ's revelation we know He is a divine Person, the third Person of the Trinity. The characteristic of the Spirit is to be a strength

Second week

that pushes and moves. It is like the wind that blows, or oil that makes muscles flexible and assures that the gears don't jam. It is a Spirit that hovers over the waters and fills all that it dampens with life. That is why it is characteristic of the Spirit to unblock our paths and to set our lives in motion so that we may go to God.

We have mentioned two names of the Spirit that help us to understand his mission. He is wind, and he is oil. We can compare our journey to that of a sailor that plies the seas. The wind fills the sails of the boat and pushes it so that it moves forward. On the other hand, the oil prepares the wood of the boat so that it can throw into the sea. This way it allows the boat to be flexible, and allows the keel to break through the waves and open a path through the waters.

Like the sailor, we need this Spirit who is wind and oil. We do not move in life because we lack the wind that impels our boat from behind. Our past paralyzes us: the many fears, the grudges we hold, the lack of forgiveness. But let us allow the Spirit to come; let us learn to leave the past in the hands of God, in his pardon and mercy; let us recognize that all we have is a gift from him; and we will find the wind filling our sails.

The same thing is true for our future. We cannot advance because we are paralyzed by fear and uncertainty. But let us allow the oil of the Spirit to come. Let us have confidence in the love of God, and let us put our tomorrows in his hands. Then our boat will be flexible and will make its way through the ocean.

If the wind blows on our sails and the oil steeps into the wood of our craft, we will be able to live in the present. He who trusts in the mercy of God for the past and puts himself in the hands of God for the future can move the rudder day by day. Listen then to the cry of John the Baptist, "Be converted, prepare the way of the Lord!" and you will bear fruit.

In Advent, the Spirit offers the formula for the Christian time. As we look back, let us always see the love of the Father, who created us and watches over us. As we look forward let us contemplate his open arms, which await us. Then we will be free to move the tiller, to change our life, surrendering each moment into the arms of love.

Second week

Traveled Paths

> "In his arms he gathers the lambs... /leading the ewes with care" (Is 40:11)
>
> "Prepare the way of the LORD /make straight his paths" (Mk 1:3)

Today Advent invites us to prepare the paths of the Lord. The king arrives soon, so we must straighten the ways of our hearts. Are they well disposed? What must we do so that the Lord may come through them?

We know that there are two types of paths and therefore two ways to care for them. On the one hand, there are paved roads that are subject to wear. The more heavy vehicles travel on them, the more they deteriorate. Every so often the road rollers may come to work so the roads don't become full of potholes.

The same thing happens to the path of life. Once in a while we must asphalt our roads again. Advent is a time to do this. It is the time to ask for forgiveness, to go to confession, to make an effort to remove our vices. If we do not, our Lord cannot make the way with us at Christmas.

There is another kind of path, like the dirt roads in the country, or the paths in the mountains that go to the peak. These paths change in an opposite way from the paved roads; they deteriorate more when they are not used. They need people who transit them. Each step evens them out, checks the growth of weeds that would cover them; those who pass remove the fallen branches and throw aside the rocks. But when those paths are abandoned and no one uses them, nature reclaims them, and they cease to be paths. Instead they disappear into the uninhabited forest.

The paths of Advent are like those paths. How should we care for them? There is only one way: that we continuously use them so that they become bridges for our comings and goings. The vocation of the path is a humble one: we must allow ourselves to be stepped on and carry many infirmities. But it is the only way for the path to remain level, free of weeds and rocks, and to be ready to be traveled by the King.

We might ask ourselves then, if our life is truly a path through which persons traverse, are we a path for our brothers and sisters? For our children, for our spouse? Can they grow and become closer to God through us? Love consists not only in accepting one another as we are, but also in discovering what can be and helping the other to advance toward that goal. He who loves sees the possibility of growth in his brothers. He looks at them according to the projects of God for them, and so can help them to mature and bear fruit.

In the Gospel, God says that he will prepare the straight path so that his people will return from exile. And later he explains that the path will be he himself, because he will carry us on his shoulders, "in his arms he gathers

Second week

the lambs" (Is 40:11). He invites you now to do the same for others and to be their way. This way, through each of your brothers who pass through you, Jesus himself will be passing. And you will have a worthy path to be travelled by God when he comes at Christmas.

Sunday Year C

Learn to Return

"Led away on foot by their enemies they left you: /but God will bring them back to you /borne aloft in glory as on royal thrones" (Ba 5:6)

"Prepare the way of the LORD, /make straight his paths" (Lk 3:4)

In Advent we walk toward Christmas. We learn to await the newness of God in our lives, since often we believe that nothing can change, that our sin has become habit, and that our paths are routine. Advent is the moment to learn that God can open what has always been closed. What is the newness of his presence and strength?

There was a man who loved to walk roads on foot. He took advantage of the feast days to leave his house early and head toward nearby towns. One day he would visit a shrine; another day, a mountain site; the next, a town at the edge of the sea. When he finished his outings, he would take the train back home.

When that man was old, he boasted of knowing thoroughly all the roads and paths in the vicinity. Then one of his friends said to him, "There is one path that you have never taken on foot." The walker smiled incredulously. But his friend was right, "You have never traveled the road on the return. You do not know what it

Second week

is like to travel toward home. That is the new path that you have to discover."

Today's readings tell us something similar. To arrive at Christmas, to experience all the newness that God wants to do in our lives, we need to learn to return. We hear the cries of joy from those who return from exile. And to recognize Jesus, we must look at his precursor, John the Baptist, who repeats the message of the Old Testament.

But let us return for the moment to the story of our traveler. Although old, he was spurred by the words of his friend and decided to traverse his road from the end to home. He took the train to a place he had walked to on a hundred occasions and started to walk returning toward home. Confident, he didn't even take a map, "I am going to show my friend how wrong he is. What difference does the road have going or coming? Isn't the way well known to me!"

Returning home, the man lost his way more than once. That is because he knew the paths from going ahead, but not from looking behind him. Following a narrow path, it is not difficult to find the large highway that it meets, but from the highway it is hard to find the narrow path that breaks off from its edge.

That day our walker learned two things. First, he realized that in his long walks he had never looked back. If he would have occasionally looked behind, he would have found it easy to recognize the path from the other direction. John the Baptist reminds us that it is necessary to look back this Advent: to the gifts that God has given us, to the love that has always cared for us, and to the forgiveness given without measure.

Our pilgrim also learned that the path returning is, in its own way, a new path. We are attracted by novelty and often discount the value of the return. But the first step forward toward God is always a step back. It is the step of recognizing our sinfulness and confessing it to our Lord. And the path that follows is also a path of return. In effect, learning to return means becoming like children; for only the little ones can enter the stable. Advent is a path of service, of doing at home the most humble tasks, and taking the first step always with love.

In the midst of getting lost, the pilgrim of our story was consoled by knowing that his destination was his own home. That is why he could travel without fear. If we learn to look back, recognizing the love of God that has created us and cares for us, it will be easy to return with joy to the house of the Father, our past and everlasting home.

Second week

A Holy Way

> "A highway will be there, /called the holy way" (Is 35:8)
> "They...lowered him on the stretcher through the tiles into the middle in front of Jesus (Lk 5:19).

The prophet Isaiah tells us today that a holy way will be opened. Advent is the time of ways—ways that take us to Bethlehem and are full of people at Christmas time. We walk too, since life is for man a pilgrimage. Gonzalo de Berceo told us thus,

> All we who live and travel on our feet
> —unless we are in prison or on our sickbed—
> we are all pilgrims that traverse a path.

Maybe we dream of a sure path, a wide path that takes us to our destination in safety. How different, however, is the path that is before us! There is before us a new day, or a lifetime, and it is proper that we need to discover our route every day. This path needs to be opened and to be made every day as we walk along it. The paths of our life are not yet level. We must level them with our falls and risings; we must explore the paths first and travel them later.

We find a good example of this in today's Gospel reading. The friends of the paralytic opened a new way; they invented the way to reach Jesus. Who would have thought of breaking in through the roof? Many times God

Monday

is hidden, and he allows us to look for him. He does this to kindle in us the desire to find him, so that we will use the means at hand. He does it because as we travel along our way, we grow.

Today God will open for us a holy way. That does not mean that he will remove our obstacles swiftly or that a highway will appear in our jungle. The jungle will continue to be a jungle, and it will always be necessary to have a machete on hand to open the way. It is good that it is so, for God wants us to grow as we walk. And only the paths that we open with sorrow and effort, putting into them all that we are, are able to make us greater. It is the glory of God to hide our paths, and it is the glory of man to discover them.

Even so, God will open a holy way for us, a great route for our steps. How can that be, as we have said that we must invent new ways each day? He will do it, walking by our side; the same God will lead the pilgrim, and so, no traveler will lose his way, "nor fools go astray on it.../It is for those with a journey to make, and on it the redeemed will walk. /Those the LORD has ransomed will return" (Is 35:8-9). His love in us, his companionship, and the desire in us to present ourselves to him to be cured, will be what guides us on the paths of Advent. That love is a new way—a way that travels through unknown sites of surrender and humility. And yet, we walk through them in total security, since Jesus, the Way in person, walks before us.

Second week

Joy, the Food for our Journey

"Comfort, give comfort to my people, /says your God" (Is 40:1)

This second week of Advent is marked by joy. The heart must be prepared for the coming of the Lord in order to receive the true joy of Christmas. "Comfort, give comfort to my people, says your God..." That is why we will listen to the parable of the lost sheep.

We know what this parable means from our point of view: God came to find us when we went astray. We were far from him amid the thickets and our thousand problems, and we see him risk dangers to save us. As St. Augustine comments, by taking the sheep upon his shoulders, he became for that sheep the way.

Sometimes we forget to meditate from the perspective of God. He does not think as much in terms of the difficulties as he thinks in terms of the joy of finding the sheep. C. S. Lewis converted to Christianity because of a surprising and inexplicable joy that he experienced at times. Things are overflowing with joy because they have been created by a joyous God in an act of joy. Some of that joy is what the Lord is inviting us to cultivate in these days of Advent.

Tuesday

There is a spiritual illness that the Christian tradition has called acedia. It consists in not being able to glad when good things happen,—when God gives us gifts that are themselves fountains of joy. Dante Alighieri, while going through hell, finds those condemned by acedia; they are submerged in a lake of black mud, and they describe their situation in these words, "When we were alive and we enjoined the pleasant air, joyous with the sun, we were sad; and now, in the black lake, we remain sad." These persons, surrounded by the air of creation and pierced by the light of the sun, were incapable of joy. Their sin was in their blindness, in their resistance to the joy that surrounded them and asked to enter into their lives. Their punishment is the one that they chose: the sadness that they nurtured inside has conquered them outside and surrounds them as the mud of the sad puddle.

It is true that many times it does not depend on us whether sad or happy events occur. It is also true, however, that we can fight for joy and for discovering the happy signs under the melancholic blankets in our life. A rabbinical teaching says that on the day of judgment God will ask for accounts for all the joy that we wasted. It is necessary to have a generous heart to be happy and to forget our own woes, which at times push us into pessimism and self-pity. A generous heart is needed to open the windows to the joy of creation, of life, and to the humble joy of sharing the commonplace. From that perspective we understand these words of Mother Teresa

Second week

of Calcutta, "When we are sad it is basically because we have denied Jesus something."

At Christmas we will ask how can there be sadness when life has just been born? During Advent we contain that joy; on Sundays we do not sing the Gloria. The purpose is to get us ready to receive the inner joy of God.

Wednesday

The Starred Circle

"They will soar as with eagles' wings; /They will run and not grow weary" (Is 40:31)
"I will give you rest" (Mt 11:28)

We started this Advent knowing that is a nighttime route. The weariness is not as heavy as the darkness. We take in hand many affairs for which we do not know the future, and we learn to walk with them. So, in this nighttime route, the clear night permits us to see the sky, and the countless stars of which Isaiah speaks. In them is inscribed the order of the universe and the regular circle of the constellations. To the ancient people, it seemed possible to read in them their destiny—their luck and the future of each individual and each group. From their perspective, they doubted that there was truly freedom for humanity; everything seemed ordained by the signs of the Zodiac and their horoscopes.

The prophet, however, proclaims hope. Yahweh, he says, is the true master of the stars, the only one who has in his hands the path of time. That is why it is possible to await novelty. The constant cycle of the seasons that succeed each other in their routine, the turning to infidelity and sin of the people, the circle of evil that seems to demand ever more violence and that has Israel held prisoner in a foreign land; to all these cycles it is

Second week

possible to set limits and to make them explode—proclaiming that something new will come, an unexpected return to Jerusalem, a glorious reconstruction of the Temple.

We also travel in our circles. In the offense that calls for another offense; in the vice in which we fall today, tomorrow, and after. Then the good news resounds. We can break our cages, and escape to the heights, open way above the stars.

In precisely this is the virtue of hope. It is born when we realize that only action from on high can break the frontiers and reach a new height. Hope is always a desire to achieve things that are above us, which are beyond our possibilities. That is why we must rely on someone that is bigger than we are, someone who will raise us where we cannot raise ourselves, higher than the starred sky.

That is why hope grows with suffering and weakness. It is only when our plans fail and we fall under the weight of pain, that we understand that we are advancing in a circle that we cannot break on our own. On the contrary, those who have never tasted the dust have the illusion that they are traveling at a great rate, moved from desire to desire. They do not understand that they are only dancing to the rhythm of the stars. "Take my yoke upon you," says Jesus in today's Gospel. Paradoxically, it is taking on a load that raises us up. Those who embrace that load, we can say with Isaiah, will have wings like the eagle, will walk without tiring, and will run without fatigue.

Wednesday

St. Ignatius of Antioch expressed it beautifully as he contemplated the star of Christmas. In Bethlehem appears a star superior to all, a new star. The laws of destiny are broken by it; a road is opened in the skies; the horoscopes that imprisoned us lose their power, and we are freed of the superstitions that did not allow us to grow.

If it is possible to rise above the stars, if it is possible to soar with the eagles' wings, it is because God himself has come to share our suffering. He has broken the circle first by coming to us, and so we can be elevated toward him. In rising, he has shared our yoke; he has taken our cross and has transformed it into an occasion of love. We have understood how much he searched for us and the great love that God has for the world. When someone has loved so, who will not return that love? The magic circle is surpassed by another circle—the circle of love that is in reality a spiral, because it makes us rise above all, toward fullness.

Second week

Making Oneself Small

"Fear not, O worm Jacob, /O maggot Israel" (Is 41:14)
"The least in the Kingdom of heaven is greater than he" (Mt 11:11)

Jesus praises John the Baptist, his precursor. His figure reappears in our Advent. But now the Lord adds that the smallest in the kingdom of heaven is greater than he.

This phrase of Jesus's is mysterious. Doesn't John belong to the Kingdom? Maybe one must say that the Kingdom is for small people, is the place for the little ones; there the law of size is inverted, and those that are of small measure become giants, and the giants, to see further, must climb on the shoulders of the dwarfs.

This kingdom, the kingdom of the little ones, is on the path toward Christmas. In all the other paths of life we are asked to ascend, even to ascend high mountains. In our route of Advent, it is backwards. Advent deals with a descending path, in which there is no increase; we must become small to enter the very low door of the basilica of Bethlehem.

I remember a book that I read as a boy in which there was a character who could do something curious: he would contradict the laws of perspective. When the man in the story was far in the horizon, he looked like a giant, and was frightful. But then, upon nearing, he shrank until it could be seen that he was an inoffensive man, with the same stature as everyone else.

What does it mean to make oneself small? In the first place, it is an invitation to simplicity and sincerity. We go through life trying to appear large, like walking on stilts. "Fear not, O worm Jacob, O maggot Israel," the prophet tells us (Is 41:14). He invites us to get rid of the useless boast and of our vanity. Christmas is a place of encountering the family, in which God speaks to us in the warmth of a personal friendship. It is best to walk in truth before him.

Love tends to make itself small, to give room to the loved one. "Love is not pompous, it is not inflated" (1 Cor 13:4). Advent is the path of God toward man—the path in which the Lord becomes small until he has the smallness of a newborn babe in Bethlehem. "Incline your heavens and descend." God likes to descend from his height, being, as he is, the highest. He is attracted by the small. "The afflicted and the needy seek water in vain, /their tongues are parched with thirst. /I, the LORD, will answer them; /I, the God of Israel, will not forsake them. /I will open up rivers on the bare heights..." (Is 41:17-18).

Let us ask the Lord to give us the desire to be small, "humbly regard others as more important than yourselves," (Phil 2:3) is the rule of all Christian life. If we lived it, the miracle would come. Since nobody is afraid of the little ones, even the poorest would find a place where they could take refuge; the brother would be at peace with us, and Jesus would have an inn in Bethlehem.

Friday

Cold or Heat at Christmas

"We played the flute for you, but you did not dance, we sang a dirge but you did not mourn" (Mt 11:17)

The readings today bring us to a crossroads. The path of Advent seems to divide into two. There are those who, like the magi, look for the star of Bethlehem so they may adore the Child; others, like Herod, aspire for the same star, but for different reasons. The Psalm warns us, "the LORD watches over the way of the just, /but the way of the wicked vanishes" (Ps 1:6). And the first reading tells us, "If you would hearken to my commandments, /your prosperity would be like a river..." (Is 48:18).

In the Gospel, we hear the lament of Jesus himself. John the Baptist came on a path of penance; the Son of Man, on the contrary, eats and drinks. It all corresponds to the wisdom of God and to each one is entrusted a particular way of acting. But the Pharisees are incapable of discovering the divine way in one or the other. What does the Lord then exclaim? "We played the flute for you, but you did not dance, we sang a dirge but you did not mourn" (Mt 11:17). Jesus is sorrowful for their frigid response. Isn't he telling us what can happen to us at the arrival of Christmas?

It happens that God, full of passion for man, cannot pull joy or sorrow out of our hearts. He tries everything in a holy night full of contrasts: the cold of the snow and the warmth of the Child, the greatness of God and the smallness of the manger, the rich angels and the poor St. Joseph, Mary mother and Mary virgin...In Bethlehem one can laugh and cry; one can be sorrowful for the misery of so many brothers or the sins that distance us from God and jump for joy for the saving grace that the same Lord brings. What cannot occur in Bethlehem is indifference before so many great things.

Quevedo described human love thus,
> Fainting, daring, infuriated,
> rough, tender, liberal, evasive,
> encouraged, mortal, dead, alive,
> loyal, traitor, cowardly, spirited,
> not finding beyond the good center and repose,
> showing joyful, sorrowful, humble, arrogant,
> annoyed, brave, fugitive,
> satisfied, offended, jealous...

The contrary of that is sung in the sad carol of the inn keeper by Luis López Anglada,
> Lord, I have nothing
> that I can give to you,
> my soul is closed,
> empty, hollow, as a bored rock...
> If you want the cold, yes;
> I am he who did not
> open the inn to you.

"We played the flute for you, but you did not dance, we sang a dirge but you did not mourn." St. Peter Chrysologus, in preparation for Christmas, reminds us that we must light our desire for the arrival of that day. The saint asks himself, how can our heart aspire to see God, whom all the earth cannot contain? That desire is impossible, disproportionate. And yet that thought does not satisfy the one who loves. "The law of love does not worry about what will be, what should be, what can be. Love does not reflect, does not use reason, does not know moderation...Love is inflamed by a desire that leads it toward things forbidden to man" (*Sermon* 147). And love will find the reply; at Christmas Eve it will be possible to see God...

"We should not sleep the holy night away." So sings an ancient carol. We can do everything but to sleep the drowsiness of the soul, except to pass indifferent before the mystery of God. To travel on the road of Advent means to prepare to sing, either laughing or crying, at Christmas.

Second week

The Hope of Creation

> "How awesome are you, Elijah! ... /You were destined…in time to come /to put an end to wrath before the day of the Lord" (Si 48:4.10)
>
> "Elijah will indeed come and restore all things" (Mt 17:11)

The readings today continue the cycle dedicated to the precursor, John the Baptist. As we unfold his figure, Advent presents to us the tension of waiting which grows each day. It has been Jesus himself who has been explaining the mystery of John: the prophet who proclaimed justice in the Jordan and announced that God would bring a greater justice; the one greatest among those born of women that proclaimed the Kingdom to the little ones...

In today's reading, Jesus resumes his ministry comparing John to Elias, "He is Elijah, the one who had to come." In this form the figure of John is framed by the history of the people of Israel. In John one sees the patriarchs, the prophets, and the just ones of the Old Testament. We hear then that John not only announces the hope of each person, but the hope of the people, of the whole of humanity, of the entire cosmos.

The figure of Elijah reminds us of something very important about true hope. We do not walk alone, and we cannot wait alone. Ours must be the hope of all who walk along our path.

In reality, if we are capable of truly waiting, it is precisely because we are united—because we walk together down through the generations, in our common history. Parents, for example, wait through their sons: they ask that their sons give fruit corresponding to the seeds that they have planted with their paternal love and dedication. But the children also hope in their parents when they look toward them for the security that they need to walk into the future, and when they ask for support and guidance for their road of life.

This community of hope is what we live in as the Church, the Body of Christ. When one member hopes, the whole body hopes as we could say paraphrasing Saint Paul. And that hope is extended to all of creation. When Jesus described for his disciples the mystery of the time that was remaining for his final coming, he used the image of a woman about to give birth (cf. Jn 16:21). Saint Paul, in the eighth chapter of the letter to the Romans, speaks also about all creation suffering the pains of birth as it awaits the birth of the son of God. Our personal Advent is therefore united to the Advent of each small thing in the world that surrounds us. Let us look around us with amazement and feel the beat of hope that slowly ripens toward the complete birth of Christ in every being.

That is why a Christian does not look down on the small hopes of history. Those are the hopes of each day for which people tire—the ones that appear reflected in our ordinary conversations, in our newspapers, and on television...All of them have value if they know how to unite themselves to the great hope, the kingdom that God wants to establish in the world. The first Christians described their mission as a sowing of seeds in the world. These seeds would give fruit in time and make history grow toward God. The Christian must sow the new seed that will make each of the hopes of man grow toward God on high.

Mary, the woman of this Advent, is the icon of this hope in communion. She is the mother that gives birth and prepares thus for the definitive end, as attested by Elijah.

Manuel Benitez has described with simple verses how all creation unites its voice to the yes response of Mary and prepares for the birth of Jesus,

> When She said yes,
> the rosemary said no;
> I do not deserve
> that the diapers of God
> dry on my branches...

The poet explains later that each little thing started to repeat in its way the yes of Mary. For example the animals that were staying in the stable,

> When she said yes,
> the small donkey
> tested its warmest breath
> for a wintry night
> by the manger of God.

Saturday

(...)
All the small things
started to put
their part in the redemption
when She said yes.

Surrounded by this magnificent choir, it will also be possible for us to start to perform our small but essential part.

Third Week

Sunday Year A

The Joys of the Sad One

"The desert and the parched land will exult" (Is 35:1)
"The poor have the good news proclaimed to them" (Mt 11:5)

Time is dragging. When night came over us and we started walking, there was the novelty of the news, and the hope of a brand new road. And as Christmas approaches, we will gaze at the empty manger, awaiting with eagerness the imminent surprise. But now, halfway to Advent, we feel the fatigue and weariness. "Are you the one who is to come, or should we look for another?" That is the question that John the Baptist asked from his prison cell.

Jesus gives a clear answer, "hear and see," and then, "Go and tell John what you hear and see." Before the temptation of fatigue and becoming disheartened, the Lord is saying: open your eyes and realize all that is happening in front of you; understand the joy of what happens when you encounter me, even if it is a joy that is mixed with tears. Today, *Gaudete* Sunday (the Sunday of "rejoice," as the antiphon says at the beginning of Mass), we remember joy as the appropriate dress of Advent.

There are many types of joy. There is, for example, the joy of receiving unexpected good news, and also the joy of relief that one can feel when an old obstacle impeding our way has been removed. Also our Advent has a special type of rejoicing: the joy of hope. That is the joy for something that we still do not possess totally although we have the first fruits. It is the joy of the new sprout that promises the fruit; the joy of the woman that awaits a child; the joy of a fresh morning that promises a radiant sun. We could say that it is the delight for the light that already illuminates our night journey. The eyes of hope are capable of discerning in the darkness the light that anticipates the coming of the day.

The joy of Advent is the joy of the one that does not yet have the full of what he longs for. He perceives a special light that is combined with darkness. The readings for today do not forget it. That is why along with joy, they present the hardness of waiting.

How can we be happy in spite of our sufferings and pains? How is joy present in spite of so many uncertainties and the darkness that surrounds us? When we consider our lives, we see that often there is a mix of joys and sufferings. We try to make the joys overtake the pains so that we have a positive balance, and then we think we have found a solution. But the answer is not sufficient because we never achieve the fullness we yearn for. It is as though we have a light that is full of shadows, and not the perfect day full of sunlight that we wish to enjoy. That is why we must look for a better answer, the one that Jesus gives us.

What Jesus's answer to those sent by John is that the poor are evangelized and receive the good news. He is telling them that the path of suffering that John is now going through, the prison and pain, are in reality a font of joy, because they are the means by which we reach God. Only through them do we learn about true joy—the joy of love, the only joy that never ends.

In this way Jesus teaches us the art of transforming sorrow into joy, of feeding the fire of our joy with the wood of our sorrows. If we act this way, we will never lack for laughter and consolation on our way. Think of trees, capable of transforming dung into sap that nourishes its juicy fruit. Or of the water treatment plant that receives a river of dirty water contaminated by heaviness, tiredness, and lacking in hope...and yet with this same water produces a clear spring, the pure spring of a mountain, fruitful enough to water our fields. In Advent we learn the art of drawing out joy from everything that happens in our life; of converting everything—good or bad—into an act of thanksgiving and blessing.

The poet Antonio Machado describes a dream, speaking about the heart as it were a hive,

> The golden bees
> were making in it,
> out of the old bitterness
> sweet honey and soft wax

If we complain that there is little joy in the world with which to water our fields, hope has inexhaustible reserves. It knows how to transform those bitter moments—of which there are plenty every day—into a font of sweetness. The fire of hope will never be diminished, because the wood we use to light the fire is precisely our own smallness in which Jesus has placed his seal and his promise.

Sunday Year B

The Joy of the One Who Waits

"I will rejoice heartily in the LORD... /and a garden makes its growth spring up" (cf. Is 61:10-11)
"Rejoice always" (1 Ts 5:16)

"It is better to have a joyful day with half a loaf than a sad day with pheasant." That is a saying, and it is true. Joy is important because it changes everything. To the happy person, the way seems bearable; it is not hard to work, and forgiveness happens without effort. When we are sad, on the contrary, life is heavy, and so also are our quarrels with our neighbors.

This third Sunday of Advent is *Gaudete* Sunday, the joyful Sunday. The prophet and also St. Paul tell us, "Rejoice." What is typical of this joy of Advent?

A prisoner in a concentration camp told it well. Only one day of the year, the day of the great feast, were they permitted to rest. He would reflect on it thus: there is only one day a year that is joyful, and is not the day of the feast...it's the eve of the feast. Thus is human hope. His greatest joy is in the expectation, because the feast, whatever it may be, will finally disappoint us. But the eve will not; the eve holds a promise, and our hearts can be filled with the expectation of an unlimited fulfillment.

The same happens in our lives. We are happy about what we await every day, but then, as soon as we achieve it, we are again sad because it does not fill our heart. And yet, we begin again our search every new day, because we need hope like animals need salt.

The Spanish philosopher Julian Marias defined happiness by calling it a life full of hope. In effect, building up our hope expands our lives and helps us to keep going. The one who has hope has something to both live and give oneself up for.

The figure of John the Baptist, in the time of Advent, is the figure of hope, because he symbolizes the time that precedes the moment before the great feast. But there is a difference compared to the prisoner we spoke of. In the case of John, the feast will not disappoint; the gift will exceed our expectation. He who feels disappointed with the feast of Christmas has not understood the gift that is given to us.

The joy of Advent invites us to ask: where do we seek our happiness? Money and pleasure soon disappoint us. There are, however, joys that do not end, that keep hope alive in our lives. And those joys are found first in the people that surround us. Each person, being an inexhaustible font of richness, is also an inexhaustible font of joy. If we look deeper, we will see that people always give more of themselves because their mystery is deep and rooted in the very love of God. This is the true basis of the endless joy: in those that we love, we can find the path that leads us to our end, God himself. Only the love of God can arouse and sustain a hopeful life.

The English writer Gilbert K. Chesterton recounted what happened to him as he travelled by bus. All the riders were elderly persons who were returning from their work, with weary faces because it had been a long day. Then a young mother came into the bus with her young son. He was a warm child that was continuously smiling and making a racket. At once, the atmosphere in the bus changed; the joy of the mother and child passed on to the others. The writer recounted that the same thing happens at Christmas. We are all riding tired and bored in the world's bus until Jesus and Mary come aboard, and we receive their contagious joy.

There is an icon, the Virgin of the Candle, that shows Mary with Jesus in her arms. The child has a candle in his hands, and he takes care that the flame does not go out: He protects it with his hand, and Mary also puts her hand so as to move away the breeze from the small light. This painting reveals the mystery of the joy of Advent. The day of the feast, for those who await the gifts of God, will never disappoint the expectations of the eve. The light of our hope will continue to glow as it is protected by the hand of the Child and his Mother.

Third week

The Joy of Pilgrims

> "Sing joyfully, O Israel.../the LORD has removed the judgment against you" (Zep 3:14-15)
> "I am not worthy to loosen the thongs of his sandals..." (Lk 3: 16)

The nomads of the desert are always thinking about water. There are few places where they can get provisions, which have to last them on long journeys. That is why they enjoy the day in which they arrive at an oasis, and they can celebrate the feast. There is water enough to drink abundantly, to wash away the fatigue of the long days beneath the sun.

I asked one of these nomads what were his greatest moments of joy. I expected that he would respond: those that we spent in the oasis, enjoying the water. He said, instead, "Those are not the happiest days. It is true that we can drink abundantly. But we know also that it won't last. One knows that the next day we must continue our journey and the level of water in our canteens will diminish each day, step by step."

He continued, "There is only one moment when one knows that the water will increase, that the next day there will be more water, more rest, more joy. It is the day before we arrive at the spring. That is the day of greatest poverty, when there is thirst, when fatigue is weighing us

Sunday Year C

down; however, we walk lightly knowing that the following day we surely will have more: more shade, more joy, more life."

His reply was the perfect reply for a nomad. True joy is not given by possessions, but by hope. We, who are nomads throughout life, learn thus the joy of Advent that the readings today recall for us. "Shout for joy, O daughter Zion," sings the prophet. It is not the joy of the one that has many things, but the joy of the one that knows that tomorrow he will have more, and that happiness will grow. It is the joy of hope, similar to the hope of the mother who, like Mary during those days, awaits the birth of a child.

During our journey as nomads, the true water that we need for our life is love. It sometimes happens that we feel that love is used up as we journey. Love seems to get old and worn out. We don't love our husbands as we once did; we see our wives full of defects; we are grown, and it is becoming more difficult to love our parents...

Can you imagine what would be the best news that we could give our nomad friend? It would be that he could take with him the spring. If from the bottom of his canteen a spring would rise, he would know that there would always be more water. However much one would drink, the spring would never dry.

That is what is happening in the Gospel today. John the Baptist says that he is not worthy to loosen the thongs of Jesus's sandals. According to the tradition of the Old

Testament, it is a way to say that Jesus is the bridegroom that announces the joy of the wedding banquet. The one who has the bridegroom with him knows that love will grow because the wedding day nears; the wedding day that will seal an eternal covenant.

Advent invites you to wait. Faith tells us of the arrival in our lives of the very spring of love: Jesus, the bridegroom. The joy of Advent is enormous, because we will be able to take with us, within our canteens, love itself. If we put him in our marriage, in our family, then the water will never cease; each day will be full of more love, more patience, and more strength for the journey we take together. Tomorrow there will be more, and that is the joy of the pilgrim. "Shout for joy, O daughter Zion!... /The LORD, your God, is in your midst."

Monday

Seeing From Afar

"I see him... I behold him... /a star shall advance from Jacob" (Nm 24:17)
"By what authority are you doing these things?" (Mt 21:23)

The last part of Advent is nearing, which will start on December 17. We will change gear, as we should change to the overdrive for our hopefulness. In this first part of Advent, the first reading considered the people of Israel and the promise of great consolation. When the seventeenth arrives, we will start hearing about the coming of the Messiah. The liturgy will then show us a close-up of Jesus. We will then see how the joy and happiness that was promised to Israel was none other than Christ himself, the Lord.

Thus, today's readings, are still speaking about the people of Israel. They speak of the prophet Balaam, a man of unique destiny. A certain king summoned Balaam to curse the people of Judah from the mountain. He saw at his feet the tribes encamped, and the monarch asked him to prophecy woes on them. But Balaam was incapable of doing that; while he wanted to curse, only blessings came out from his mouth. "How goodly are your tents, O Jacob; /your encampments, O Israel."

Balaam is the man who sees, "I see him, though not now; I behold him, though not near," and, "The utterance of Balaam... /the utterance of the man whose eye is true..." At this time in our Advent journey, we are still traveling from afar, and the night is still dark. In this night we are invited to see, to be persons of vision.

It is said that a good business person is one who has vision; that is, one who can see things not as they are today, but as they will be when he has transformed them. Then he can communicate that idea, and sell his vision. He is capable of putting it into effect and making it a reality. Something similar happens now. But what we are asked is to have the vision of God, "The utterance of Balaam... /of one who sees what the Almighty sees." That is to say, we are taught to see how things will be when the grace of God has permeated them; when he has calmed our sadness and dried up our tears, and when he has changed our heart and given us wings to fly. Only the one who has that vision can make it reality.

Balaam is like that. Tradition sees him as a precursor of the three Magi, who also studied the stars. The most famous part of his prophecy is, "I see him, though not now; /I behold him, though not near: /A star shall advance from Jacob, /and a staff shall rise from Israel."

So the third week of Advent advances and takes us for a moment to the last stage, which will start on December 17. We are given the announcement of the coming of Jesus. This way we are being told: your vision should be focused on him; he is the "vision of the Almighty,"

Monday

because he is the star. In Jesus we can foresee our future happiness.

The Pharisees in the Gospel couldn't understand it. When the Jesus asked them, "Where was John's baptism from? Was it of heavenly or of human origin?" they would not answer, because they did not think that John came from God. If they had admitted that, they would have to accept Jesus, whom John preceded and announced. If they had had vision, they could have discerned in the coming of John, and, as in any other event, the one who comes from God, Jesus Christ. The vision of Advent means looking to the future relying on Jesus, seeing how he is going to build our lives according to his life. Let us be then, people of vision, capable of projecting ahead of our steps the footprints of Christ. We will thus walk unafraid toward that which we can only discern from afar.

Third week

A Road for the Few

> "I will leave as a remnant in your midst /a people humble and lowly /Who shall take refuge in the name of the LORD" (Zep 3:12)
>
> "Tax collectors and prostitutes are entering the Kingdom of God before you" (Mt 21,31)

We know it already; there will be a few of those who on Christmas Eve will take what they have on hand as a present and go to the manger.

Zephaniah tells us today so we will not deceive ourselves, "I will leave as a remnant in your midst /a people humble and lowly /Who shall take refuge in the name of the LORD." The humble and lowly are the shepherds and the drummer boy of the Spanish carol, and also the magi with their gold, frankincense, and myrrh. Not much compared to all the inhabitants of Jerusalem who will remain at home. The humble and lowly remnants are the infants of Bethlehem, but Herod's soldiers will be greater in number and stronger.

In the Gospel Jesus speaks also about that remnant. It won't be that of the proud or those who recognize themselves as good. The Pharisees did not receive the message of John the Baptist, but the publicans and prostitutes did. Behold that remnant of people is humble and lowly. They are the people who can be amazed to see

Tuesday

the surprise of a tiny God. The first lesson that we learn from the remnant is the humility of the one that confesses himself as sinner.

The second lesson from the remnant is to know how to support one another along our journey, for we are few. St. Teresa of Avila commented, "The service of God is so scarce, that it is necessary to lean on one another, those who serve, to make progress...and if one begins to give himself to God, there are so many that gossip, that it is necessary to find companions to defend oneself, until one is strong enough" (*Life* 7:22).

Thus is our path of Advent; thus is our Christian life. Few will go to the manger; most will prefer to turn their backs. Is this reason for pessimism? Not at all! Zephaniah speaks of the remnant as a blessing from God. Further yet, "the remnant of the remnant," the place where the holy ones will gather, is the stable of Bethlehem. It is Joseph and Mary, and yes, definitely, Jesus.

And thus we arrive to the third lesson about the remnant. Jesus belongs to the remnant, and he is a true friend. As St. Teresa tells us, he can be at our back and defend us. The saint continues, "There were many friends to help me fall; but I found myself so alone getting up, that I am amazed that I wasn't always fallen, and I praise God's mercy, that it was he alone who gave me a hand" (*Life* 7:22). That remnant, says the prophet, will serve God "under the same yoke." It is the yoke of Jesus, "Come to me, for my yoke is easy and my burden light."

Third week

And so we reach the fourth lesson of the remnant: the remnant is called to be more than the remnant; it is called to be yeast. Someone said, "The Church is something of few for the many." Pope Benedict XVI, in his encyclical *Spe Salvi,* affirms that the hope of the world is always in the hands of a few that can give life to the rest (*Spe Salvi* 15). The remnant is for all. The few that arrive in Bethlehem will leave Bethlehem and make of the whole world a great stable.

Wednesday

Hope in the Shoot and Hope in the Fruit

> "I am the Lord, there is no other" (Is 45:6)
> "Should we look for another? (Lk 7:20)

John the Baptist, the witness of Advent, man of hope, also had his dark days. Arrested by Herod, who wished to silence his courageous denunciation, he suffered the night and silence of jail. Those are difficult moments for his disciples also. Then a question arises from them; if Jesus is the liberator of Israel, why this seeming failure? Are the powerful continuing to triumph at the expense of the people of God?

The disciples of the Baptist then take a question to Jesus. It is one that rises in every person who has waited once and again and has come across disenchantment, "Are you the one that is to come, or should we look for another?" We have waited with hope many times and many times it has proven to be a false hope. We pursue a desire that promised happiness—it was a perfect job, a new house, an unexpected prize. Everything has gone on disappointing us, and we have been told over and over that this is not it. Then we must wait for someone else. And the stubborn hope takes the road again; it is determined to await the definite one, if it exists...

Are you the one that is to come, or should we look for another? The desolation of John in jail teaches us to distinguish between true and false hope—that which must look for another and the hope that does not defraud, hoping against hope.

For our answer it will be helpful to understand that there are two types of hope. There are the hopes of the shoot and the hopes of the fruit. The first hopes are messengers of novelty. A new flower, a small miracle has been born in the desert. There is an epiphany of light, of newness that encourages us to start again on our path. The spark of hope has been lit.

But that is not definitive hope. It can be a flower for a day, but later does not produce a delicious fruit. The hope of the shoot needs to convert into the hope of the fruit. The leaves grow, and the light not only surrounds the plant from outside, but it starts to inhabit within it. The chlorophyll is doing its work: the luminous energy enters the delicious juice of the fruit. An inseparable bond has been shaped between the light and the plant.

All hope starts by being a shoot; only true hope is capable of becoming a fruit. All hope is a ray of sunlight that attracts and blinds us; only true hope is light, which has entered within us to make us grow toward it and can transform us into light.

That is why patience is a necessary ingredient of hope. It is not necessary to go under the radiant light to break out into new flowers. But it is necessary to come to an agreement with the light, to allow the rays to enter the plant and put their glory into the fruit.

Wednesday

Now you can distinguish between types of hope. There are hopes that show as a bright light, but do not develop any further. There is another hope that lives in friendship, in family, in fatherhood and motherhood, and it is a hope that starts as a shoot and does produce fruit. It is the hope of the one eager to receive humbly the light, and to accept it to oneself.

"Should we look for another?" John's disciples ask Jesus. "I am the Lord, there is no other"—Yahweh says in the first reading. The people of Israel were suffering a great crisis at that time. Exiled, they had to learn to discover in their God the Creating God, the God above all other gods, who continues to be God even though his temple and his standard have been humiliated. The hope of fruit is born then at the cry of "there is no other." Those sent by the Baptist also learn that. The hope of Jesus is born in the poverty of those who know they are blind and allow the light to illuminate them in their inner selves. That is why the Teacher responds, "The poor have the good news proclaimed to them."

We should not look for another, but we must continue awaiting him; awaiting that he will enter within you and make you grow toward him. That is the hope that does not disappoint, because God has shed his love on our hearts to make himself our friend, and he is one of those friends we yearn more for.

Third week

A Return Path

"The LORD calls you back" (Is 54:6)
"You preserved me from among those going down to the pit" (Ps 30:4)

There is a big difference between the going path and the returning path. Even though the curves and the distance are the same, one walks the path with a different attitude, as the destination is different. In one direction there may be the novelty of unknown vistas; in the other, the home that is familiar. We must today meditate that the path that takes us to Bethlehem is often a path of returning. Well informed sources assure us that that the prodigal son traversed it.

We know that Christmas is a time to return to the familiar home. An old commercial of a Christmas candy said, "Return home for Christmas." But here we speak of another type of returning. St. Augustine says that we often travel on the journey of life far from the Lord. And so we travel paths that take us nowhere. Sometimes we ask, "Is it possible to return?" And if it looks like it is not worthwhile, then we have no energy to undo our steps...

In ancient times a strange penance was given to pilgrims: two steps forward, one back, two steps forward, one back...That way they learned something important about the road of life. One needs courage to take a step forward after having taken steps backward and to recognize that we have fallen and then return to the Lord. Often more courage is needed to undo our steps than to explore new directions.

God tells us in today's first reading that it is possible to return, "The shame of your youth you shall forget, /the reproach of your widowhood no longer remember. /For he who has become your husband is your Maker... /The LORD calls you back, /like a wife forsaken and grieved in spirit." Christmas means that it is possible to start anew, to undo the journey, no matter how far we find ourselves from him. There is more. Isaiah continues, "For a brief moment I abandoned you, /but with great tenderness I will take you back. /In an outburst of wrath, for a moment /I hid my face from you; /But with enduring love I take pity on you, /says the LORD, your redeemer." It is as if, rather than us turning back to God, it is God who comes to us.

During this Advent we hear the response. Before being the journey of a man, Advent is the journey of God. He has desired to travel out of love for the lost lamb. Christmas means that God pursues man, that he follows him everywhere, and that he advances and retreats with him. This journey goes through the stable at Bethlehem. God makes it easy for you; he nears you, and he saves you from thousands of steps backward.

We have the best news: God returns to your home at Christmas.

Third week

The Baptist in Advent

"John was a burning and shining lamp" (Jn 5:35)

The third week in Advent has been the week of the Baptist. John reminds us what the challenge of Advent is: to recognize the Christ when he arrives. In effect, it is useless to await him, or walk toward him, if you are not able to recognize him later when he is in front of you. He will go by you, and you would not remember to address him. That is why John, he who discovers Jesus and points to him, has been giving clues for the miracle of that vision, teaching how to recognize the Savior.

This difficulty in recognizing the Messiah showed up mostly when we heard the disciples of the Baptist questioning Jesus, to whom he answered, "Blessed is the one who takes no offense at me." This way we are reminded that what we will see at the end of Advent will surprise our eyes; what we will find will be different from our expectations, and we may be tempted to be disappointed and thus to give up.

Jesus offered us a guideline to counter the temptation when he responded to the trick question of the Pharisees: Where was John's baptism from? Was it of heavenly or of human origin? The Master knows well; the baptism of John comes from above, as well as everything that can bring newness and meaning to our existence. Looking

Friday

upward, that's the only way to accustom our sight so that we can recognize Jesus. The one who opens his eyes to the divine presence in ordinary things, in the midst of his work and family, will know how the Savior of the world is born.

On the other hand, we heard Jesus accusing the unbelieving Pharisees that the prostitutes believed in the Baptist, unlike them. And John reminds us that to prepare the way is to confess oneself small and sinful. "First comes the confession, later love," St. Augustine said (*Commentary no the Letter of St. John* 1:6). To recognize Christ we must dare to first recognize our own weakness.

This sign of poverty was the one John received from his disciples who were sent to Jesus: the poor, the small are evangelized. That is the secret; we must become small to be able to see the little light of the manger. And we must also recognize Jesus in the small steps, so that later we can find him in the larger ones. For God is always coming to where the ordinary, being simple and poor, open the doors for him.

Today the Gospel refers again to the Baptist. Jesus says, "I have testimony greater than John's." It is the testimony of the Father. As we have seen, John already pointed to the Father with his message; he announced the Creator God who sent the prophets of the Old Testament and that way arranged the coming of his Son. To look at the Father is to recognize that Jesus will come from heaven, but also that he grows from the earth, making his way through the prophets of the Old Testament until culminating in the Baptist, his precursor. In that way John taught Israel to recognize Jesus from his own path.

The last lesson is finding Jesus in the steps we have taken, in the footprints of yesterday in which his presence passed us by unrecognized. We will become used to treasuring our memories of the coming of God through our years. Even in times when we didn't see that he was acting, maybe we will now recognize him in his divine mercy when we glance back. And so we will train our eyes so that when he comes we can shout, "Behold the Lamb of God who takes away the sin of the world!" (Jn 1:29)[*]

---

[*] TN: There are no readings for the Saturday of the third week. We will be in the weekdays of Advent from December 17 to December 24.

Fourth Week

Sunday Year A

The Path After the Path

"The gospel about his Son" (Rom 1:3)
"And they shall name him Emmanuel, which means 'God is with us'" (Mt 1:23)

The readings today are an immediate preparation for the mystery of the Nativity. The crown of Advent is complete; the fourth candle is lit. It is like saying that this is all the light that what we, humans, can provide. The rest will be the light of God, lit by him, at his cost and with his luminous strength. The fifth candle can only be lit by him. We may wonder in what way will this light be special?

The first surprise is that the light, although lit by God, will provide light in the same way as our lights, in our own way, using our wax. "The gospel about his Son, descended from David according to the flesh..." (Rom 1:3) St. Paul tells us today. The fifth candle, the candle of the Nativity, will not clash with the ones we have been lighting as we were making the path of this Advent.

Yet it will be different, truly. St. Paul concludes, "Descended from David according to the flesh, but established as Son of God in power according to the Spirit of holiness through resurrection from the dead" (Rom 1:4). The mention of the Spirit indicates the newness of the light. According to the apostle, that will

Fourth week

happen in fullness in the Resurrection. But the first and second readings indicate that already Bethlehem is a new birth, made by that same Spirit, "The Virgin will conceive through the Holy Spirit."

St. Paul thus presents us with the path of Jesus, from his childbirth in the cave to the glorious rebirth at the Resurrection when his work will be culminated, and the way to heaven will be definitely opened. So our path of Advent, this path through the darkness that we started a few weeks ago, acquires new meaning as we reach this fourth Sunday of Advent. We might think that God comes to end our path, that Christmas is the end, and that we have already reached our goal. But what happens is that at the end of the path of Advent, we find ourselves on another path. In Bethlehem the path of Jesus will start, which St. Paul has summarized in a dense phrase. In the Nativity we encounter God, not in the form of a goal, but in the form of a path that wants to be traversed.

And that is precisely what we need. They tell an anecdote about the mathematician John von Neumann, the typical distracted genius. A student approached him in the hall to ask for help with a problem and he replied, "It's OK, son, as long as we can be quick, because I have a lot of work today."

"I am having trouble with this integral," said the student.

Neumann looked at the problem, "Son, the answer is two pi to the fifth power."

The young man said, "I know that already, the answer is at the back of the book. What I want to know is how to arrive at that answer."

"OK, let me see it again," answered Neumann. And after a pause he said, "Son, the answer is two pi to the fifth power."

Again the reply, "I know that, sir, my problem is how to arrive at that answer."

"But what more do you want? I have solved the problem by two different methods..."

The moral is that sharing knowledge is much more than giving the answer. It means to raise a student up so he may participate in the thinking of the professor. The path is very important. The peak of the mountain, without the rocky and steep path that endorses it, has the taste of an empty victory. Only the one who walks really earns the goal; when he arrives he will truly own it. If he has not advanced step by step, if he has received it as a sudden gift, he will not truly have arrived—although he may find himself in that place—because the goal will not truly belong to him.

God does not function like von Neumann. He prefers to tell us the way. Jesus, says St. Irenaeus of Lyon, has come to unite the beginning with the end, man with God (Irenaeus, Against Heresies, IV 20:4). He is the Way, a way that starts on earth and reaches heaven. Our route ends in Bethlehem just where the route of Jesus begins in humility.

Fourth week

We are invited to carry our questions and uncertainties, the ones with which we started Advent. We are invited to pick up our doubts and shadows of the night, the uncertain success of our projects, and hand them over to the babe of Bethlehem. We expect that he will receive them as a gift, and we will learn to walk behind him and match his stride.

Sunday Year B

The House of God is Your House

"Should you build me a house...? The LORD will establish a house for you" (2 Sam 7:5.11)
"You will conceive in your womb" (Lk 1:31)

King David had obtained a palace after much labor. Only then did he realize that God did not have a temple deserving of him: the Lord still was housed in the tent that had accompanied his people in their exodus. "How is that possible?" David said to himself, and he immediately called the prophet, "I will build a house for God with more splendor than my own palace."

The following day God responds to him. He is pleased that David is generous. But he will remind David of an essential truth. Yahweh has no need of anyone building him a house, since he is the creator of the world. And he tells David, it is I that will make you a house, the house of David. That house is a family that will continue for generations, from your descendants will be born the Messiah, the savior of all.

The history of David shows many facets of our own Advent. In the first place, it tells us that God is a God who is on the way toward us, a God that comes. He has wished to live, not in a palace or a rich house, but among shepherds, in the tent of a traveler, "He camped among us." God is always walking to be closer to you. And so,

Fourth week

the fourth candle that we light at Advent points to the fifth candle—a candle that only God himself can light with his coming. Summarized in these four candles are our efforts to build a dwelling place for Jesus arrive. But only his upcoming arrival, the fifth candle, will be able to convert the building of the manger into a true home, into a family.

This travel of God passes so near to us that it arrives at our own home. It is as though God were telling David, "Don't build me a separate house; I want your house to be my house." We are traveling in Advent, but this road doesn't disappear into a distant and strange horizon. It ends in our own living room, where our family congregates. Let's remember that the house that God is building for David is a family, the descendants from whom the Messiah will be born. The family of David will be the family of God; his house will be a common house. The prophecy will be fulfilled in the stable of Bethlehem where the Holy Family, related to David and to the whole human race, will be also the family into which the Son of God will be born.

A priest once told how he had discovered the deepest secret of Christianity. What does being a Christian mean? He had experienced it in his family while young, when praying the Rosary together at dusk. He had seen it in the different ways his father and mother prayed.

The father arrived home late from work after a hard day. For the child, the father was the supreme authority.

That is why he was impressed to see his father on his knees, quiet after his long day. And the child understood how important and great God must be for his father to leave his many responsibilities to pray in silence.

His mother prayed in a different manner. There were many children at home, and there was always much to do: fix dinner, hang up the washing, scrub the pots…She did all this while saying the Rosary. And the child understood how close to us God has come, and how small he has wished to be, since my mother is praying to him while stirring the pot or finishing the laundry!

This is the path toward Christmas: God is made man. On the one hand, he is the mysterious God. He is a God whom one must adore in silence and on one's knees because he is greater that we can imagine. On the other hand, he is a God who is close, who watches over you and protects your comings and goings, who wants you to know his very fatherly heart.

In the Gospel we hear the Annunciation to Mary. Now the promise that God made to David will be fulfilled; he will make him a house. What is that dwelling place? It is not a rich room, but the womb of a woman. There where the mother conceives, where the mystery of a family is grown, there God wants to build his dwelling place. The things of each day, the hope of an expectant spouse, the fruit of a work to which we have devoted ourselves, the forgiveness that rises in the desert of hate…All this gives testimony to the fact that our reality

Fourth week

can accept God, can become the home that God dwells in. In our house, converted into the house of God, we encounter him infinitely close and infinitely great.

Sunday Year C

Encounter From the Mother's Womb

> "The Lord will give them up, until the time /when she who is to give birth has borne" (Mi 5:2)
> "When Christ came into the world, he said:…Behold, I come to do your will" (Heb 10:5.7)
> "The infant in my womb leaped for joy" (Lk 1:44)

On this Sunday prior to Christmas, the readings invite us to place ourselves in a privileged position. It is like having a first row seat in a theater or a football match. From this place, better than any other, we can learn what Christmas is telling us. "What is this place?" The first reading tells us about the woman who is about to give birth to the Messiah. In the Gospel we see the encounter of two mothers, Elizabeth and Mary, which is also the encounter of the children that they carry in their wombs, John the Baptist and Jesus. The second reading transmits to us the attitude that the Son of God already has from the womb of his mother, "Behold, I come to do your will" Thus this is the place where the Church wishes us to arrive at the end of our Advent journey: the mother's womb.

Chesterton tells the story of a man who, bored with his home and family, travelled the world looking for happiness. He walked over hill and dale but nowhere did he find the desired joy. At the end, after months of

Fourth week

travelling, he recognized the house of his dreams. Everything looked perfect: the garden, the rooms, and the people living in it. But then the man realized that after all his travels, he had gone around the world and come back to his own house and family. The travelling had been necessary for him to appreciate anew what he already had.

The road of Advent is similar. It's about returning to the place from which we started our lives. Only the one that makes oneself like a child can enjoy Christmas. The motherly womb appears to be the goal that Advent points to: there settles the school of hope.

The nine months preceding the birth of a child are for the mother a special advent. She gives all she has, her own flesh and blood, to contribute to the development of the child. She knows, at the same time, that the child exceeds her capacity and is more than what she could herself create. She knows the child's face will always be an unexpected surprise.

The activity of hope is similar. We work for something that requires our effort and collaboration. At the same time, we understand that the work goes beyond us and that someone more powerful works within us. The hope of the mother is based, truly, in God himself, the fundament of hope. It is He who has blessed the motherly womb so that it may bear fruit. We learn here the secret of an active hope, to hope is to collaborate with him.

That is why the maternal hope is not closed on itself; it cannot be selfish. With the pregnancy, the life of the woman has become greater and has welcomed within it another life, that of her child. That is why the mother teaches us that hope is always generous: one must not hope only for oneself. Hope is always open to embrace our brothers; it becomes the hope of a friendship, of a communion. The philosopher Gabriel Marcel summarized in a few words the formula of hope, "I hope in you, for us."

Today we light the fourth candle of Advent. There remains in reality a fifth one. The crown of Advent is our poor light, made from wax that is consumed. But it prepares the arrival of the fifth candle, the candle of Christmas that only God can light. Even though we may have worked much to prepare ourselves, this last candle can only come with God. The mother, who discovers the gift of new life from on high, knows that well. God has blessed her love and has had it bear fruit. Her life is now greater, a life in communion, enlarged in her child. "I hope in you, for us."

Weekdays of Advent after December 17

December 17

He Assumed in Him the Ancient

"You, Judah, shall your brothers praise" (Gn 49:8)
"Genealogy of Jesus Christ, the son of David, the son of Abraham" (Mt 1:1)

Today, the seventeenth of December, begins a unique octave of Christmas; a reverse octave, it is the countdown until the twenty-fifth. The readings have been chosen with care. They are, if it is possible, verses more holy, because they touch on the central mystery of this time very closely. An example is the first reading from the book of Genesis. It's the blessing of Judah, followed by the blessing of all his brothers, the rest of the sons of Jacob. "The scepter shall never depart from Judah, or the mace from between his feet, until tribute comes to him." This predicts the coming of a Messiah. The first Christians interpreted it thus: the Jews, descendants of Judah, had their own rulers; in their hands remained the scepter until Jesus came. Then the Romans snatched the scepter from them.

However, the scepter did not land in the hands of the Roman armies. That ruling power was reserved to Jesus, and when it was in his hands, it was transformed. Then it was not political dominion, but the dominion of love, that of the ruler who knows how to rule hearts from the inside, not with the scourge. St. Ignatius of Loyola, in his meditation on the eternal king, calls Jesus "a King so liberal and so human," precisely because he wants to share with us, the labors, so that we may have part in his victory.

The manger of Bethlehem is converted therefore into the throne of the Lion of Judah. Romanesque art delighted in presenting the humanity of Jesus as the king in the lap of Mary. The mother is the throne of the child—a throne that testifies that Jesus is our king. Our king, not principally because he rules over us, but because he belongs to our own race, because he comes from our own family. And since he knows our affairs, our concerns, our fears, and the vicissitudes of our hearts from the inside, he is truly capable to rule with justice over our life.

In the Gospel, we will read during these next few days the account of Jesus's infancy written by Matthew and Luke. Today we start with the genealogy of our Lord according to St. Matthew. At first sight it is a boring list of ancestors with strange names. The majority of them are unknown to us. But the same monotonous recital transmits a clear message. Jesus comes with the routine of time, like many others. He assumed the anodyne of our daily life.

"Perez became the father of Hezron, Hezron the father of Ram, Ram the father of Amminadab. Amminadab became the father of Nahshon, Nahshon the father of Salmon…" We read it quietly, and it seems that we are listing the routine course of our daily hours. "Jechoniah became the father of Shealtiel, Shealtiel the father of Zerubbabel, Zerubbabel the father of Abiud. Abiud became the father of Eliakim, Eliakim the father of Azor, Azor the father of Zadok. Zadok became the father of Achim, Achim the father of Eliud…" We wake up, take a shower, we get the breakfast ready, we wait for the subway, we arrive to work…Monday, Tuesday, Wednesday, Thursday…"Abiud became the father of Eliakim, Eliakim the father of Azor, Azor the father of Zadok. Zadok became the father of Achim, Achim the father of Eliud…"

And in the midst of our journey, the final verses, "Jacob the father of Joseph, the husband of Mary. Of her was born Jesus who is called the Christ." The evangelist allows us to discern the virginal mystery of this new birth. He will explain it with the following, "This is how the birth of Jesus Christ came about…"

The scepter of Judah, the scepter that was passed from hand to hand and from descendant to descendant reaches Jesus. But it does it in a new manner, because now it is going to be transformed: the one who is born does not only belong to a family, and will not only reign over a people. There is a new fecundity, in the Spirit, and with it a miracle that will shake our daily routines. Jesus comes as one who knows us from the inside and can say the exact word that will awaken us—comes as the one who has the regal power of love. "Azor the father of Zadok.

Zadok became the father of Achim, Achim the father of Eliud…" "December the seventeenth, the eighteenth, the nineteenth, the twentieth, the twenty-first…" And at the end of the long list, the words of the poet, "Newness of all newness, and all newness: Christmas."

Joseph, Paternity and the Future

> "I will raise up a righteous shoot to David" (Jer 23:5)
> "Joseph, son of David, do not be afraid to take Mary...She will bear a son" (Mt 1:20-21).

St Mathew narrates, as Luke does, the Annunciation of Jesus. But instead of doing it from the point of view of the Virgin, he narrates the event from the point of view of Joseph. The spouse of Mary found himself with a great difficulty when he discovered that Mary was with child. What presented the doubt for Joseph? Nowadays the following interpretation is making its way through some biblical scholars: Joseph finds himself with a great mystery; he knows that Mary has conceived by the power of the Holy Spirit. What must he do? A just man, he thinks that the best thing is to distance himself, out of respect for the greatness of this birth, of this prodigious intervention of God. He will say, as the centurion who we read about on the first Monday of Advent, "I am not worthy that you should enter under my roof."

This respect of Joseph's, knowing that he is unworthy to receive the mystery, is a guiding light for us on our path toward Christmas. Joseph talks to us first of all with his silence. By not participating in the conception with Mary, he testifies that God is the father of Jesus, the original source from which the Son draws his life. So

Joseph makes it possible for a new force to appear in the story—possible that the power of God may begin to act. In this way we are reminded that first of all comes the divine action: his love and grace precede all that we can embark in. The first step in loving is always to receive the creative love with which God loves us. Obeying consists always, first of all, in being grateful.

This does not mean that Joseph would be only a passive witness. Actually, God is calling him, "Joseph, do not be afraid to take Mary." A man of few words, the readings of these days show him always acting, obeying immediately the divine mandates, making an effort to protect the child and the mother. He is always busy about the thousand small details that his mission requires.

Joseph represents therefore the mystery of paternity in the stable at Bethlehem. What is the vocation of a father, what is his mission? Every father finds himself immersed in a mystery. On the one hand, his child has changed his life, has transformed his very being; not only does he *have* a child, now he *is* a father. On the other hand, his child goes beyond him; his final origin escapes him, and also his destiny. The father realizes that he no longer controls his life as before. It has escaped him upon the arrival of his child and the new responsibility that he is now called to accept. There arises the temptation to deny the mystery in which he finds himself immersed: and so there are fathers who see a child as a mere projection of their dreams and ideals, as someone who will achieve

December 18

what they themselves did not; or some fathers just ignore the life of their child and do not want to be responsible for it.

As an antidote, there is the true paternity, of which Joseph is a witness. The real father realizes that in the center of his own being there is a life, that of his child, that he cannot truly span. His child's life is a presence that escapes him from its origin to its end. His life then appears greater than what he previously believed, open toward eternity. His work then has meaning only if he places himself in a larger horizon than his very existence, if he accepts an origin from which he comes, and a destination toward which he aims. That is, he needs to accept a fatherhood greater than his, that of God himself, with which he cooperates as father.

If this happens, if we put the future in the hands of God, if we recognize that the child exceeds our power and provisions, then a new future is opened for us. The father is converted thus into a man who knows tomorrow, and prepares the future for his family. The father becomes thus a sower of Advents, of the comings of God into the world. In this mysterious way, he collaborates with the Father from whom comes all paternity, who guides with his own hand the course of history (cf. Eph 3:14-15). The proof is in Joseph, the man that knows how to discern his tomorrow and to care always so that the child and his mother will have what they need, whether it is going to Nazareth or running away and hiding in Egypt.

We learn from Joseph, and we approach the mystery with great respect; we embrace it knowing that it is not of our own doing, "Do not be afraid to take Mary…for it is through the Holy Spirit that this child has been conceived in her." Doing so, a new horizon of fecundity is opened to us. We enter into the current of a greater paternity, that of God the Father, who gives origin and end to our steps. A future for which we can work is given to us; we are made capable of a greater mission than our own forces could give, whose final outcome is beyond our sight. And our life is made greater as a result, since it ends in the eternity of God.

December 19

The Priest in a Diaper

> "The boy shall be consecrated to God from the womb" (Jgs 13:5)
> "The whole assembly of the people was praying outside at the hour of the incense offering...Do not be afraid, Zechariah, because your prayer has been heard" (Lk 1:10-13).

The Gospel writer Luke is usually symbolized by a bull. Some say that is because of the way his Gospel begins: he presents Zechariah entering the Temple to offer the sacrifice. As every priest of Israel, the father of the Baptist mediates between God and his people. Can this image of the priest help us to prepare for Christmas?

The priesthood was the way that God made himself present to his people. The priest was the one who was separated from the rest to enter the divine mystery. This separation was necessary: it expressed the way that the transcendence of God goes beyond human imagination. The veil of the Temple isolated the zone where everybody could enter from the place reserved to the sanctity of God, where only the priest could step. After offering the sacrifice, the minister of the altar would gather back with the people, bringing to them the messages and blessings of Yahweh. Through him the divine presence became a daily one, invading all the areas of ordinary life.

In congruency with this priesthood is the birth of John the Baptist and also that of Samson, of whom the first reading speaks. These boys were born to bring the presence of God to their people, and that is why they must remain apart from ordinary life. They will not drink hard drink or eat impure food; externally they will remain at a distance from all to communicate the salvation of God to the people.

At Christmas Jesus appears also as a priest, in the line of the just ones of the Old Testament. But now the priesthood has been transformed, because what he offers is the very human existence that he shares with us. By coming into the world—we read today in the letter to the Hebrews—Jesus exclaimed, "Sacrifice and offering you did not desire, /but a body you prepared for me...Behold, I come to do your will" (Heb 10:5).

Jesus says that God has given him a body for the sacrifice. We will contemplate on the Holy Night in Bethlehem the small body of Jesus, formed by the hands of the Father in the womb of Mary. Lope de Vega was right when he imagined the stable like a church in which the Child officiated at Mass,

> You will see marvels,
> that are in the choir of the Seraphim
> and the priest in diaper.

The news is that now, with the incarnation, God not only has come down to touch the earth, but he has clothed himself with it. He has partaken of the human condition. The new sacrifice no longer requires separation, but total union with mankind. God has put himself at our own level so that he can thus raise us up to him. In effect, he now has a body and can look at the world from the inside; he is capable of transforming it with his work and offering it with his prayer, transforming the whole of it into a new temple.

That is why the mystery of sorrow that Jesus assumes is also present in Bethlehem. It is a fount of consolation for us when we must live a sad Christmas: the poverty of the cave, the cold of the night, the darkness of an uncertain future. The poet Luis Rosales paints it thus in a dialogue between God the Father and a guardian angel who, after his guard duty in Bethlehem, returns to heaven to give his novelties,

–The mule?
–Lord, the mule was tired and slept,
it can no longer give the child the breath it no longer has.
–The hay?
–Lord, the hay extends itself under the body
like a small golden but painful cross.
–The Virgin?
–Lord, the Virgin continues to cry.
–The snow?
–It continues to fall; it is cold
between the mule and the ox.

To all this enumeration of difficulties, which seem like a list of problems, God the Father responds,

–All is well.
–Lord, but
–All is well.

–Slowly the angel folded his wings and returned to the manger.

All is well, because the essential is at stake in that offering in which the Child takes the world in his hands and raises it to the Father, "Behold, I come to do your will."

December 20

The Sign of the Virgin

"Ask for a sign from the LORD" (Is 7:11)
"Behold, I am the handmaid of the Lord" (Lk 1:38)

The king Ahaz was frightened. Two great neighboring nations had allied to wage war on him. It was natural that he would look for defenses, provisions, trenches. But even so, he was unable to avoid his worst nightmares.

Then Isaiah came to him. He led him to the place where he was building up the cisterns—a key part of his resistance strategy—the place on which Ahaz was basing his hope. And then Isaiah told him prophesies from God.

The prophet invited him to dispel his fears. In the same place where he built up the cisterns, he reproached him of his little faith in God. Your enemies have no power over you, if you entrench yourself on the Almighty. "Unless your faith is firm, you shall not be firm," if you don't believe, you cannot resist the enemy.

For Ahaz, this did not seem easy. His best arguments for hope continued to be based on his reserves of water, his ramparts, and his trained warriors. Thus Isaiah offered him a sign. "Ask for a sign from the LORD, your God; /let it be deep asthe nether world, or high as the sky!" As if to say, in the depths or in the heights, God is Lord. His power goes from one end to the other. Your own confidence cannot have such deep fundaments nor your hope such high expectations.

Ahaz did not want any kind of sign. And what if God had given it? Then Ahaz would have to abandon his human support; he would possibly have to leave the plans already designed to arm the city. It did not seem to him that a sign, though it be high or low, would make it less necessary to have water, less urgent to forge spears.

"Therefore the Lord himself will give you this sign." God will decide if he will put it below the abyss or above the heavens. The Lord chooses neither: a child shall be Emmanuel, God with us. There will not be a God above, or a God below; not a deep God, nor a lofty God; it will simply be God with you, God beside you, Emmanuel.

"The virgin shall conceive and bear a son." Ahaz did not wish to embrace that sign. It is offered now to you, who are also weighed down with fears and a thousand threats. In the same manner as others, you have sought a solution; or maybe you despaired of finding one, because many times the plan has failed you. God wants to send you a sign. If you lean on it, your life will be firm.

Do not expect it from above or from below. It will appear with you, by your response to his call, there where God wants to become present and act. This is confirmed by the story of the Annunciation, where the sign of Isaiah becomes real. We find there an incredible reality: God wants to have the assent of Mary before descending to earth. He counts completely on the human yes response;

he becomes flesh by the cooperation of his creature. Saint Bernard has drawn for us, in a famous page, that brief interval between the question of the angel and the reply of Mary. As it was asked, all of creation held its breath, overcome with the importance of the moment.

This means that the sign that God gives us is only visible to those who trustingly open their hearts to him. To see him, we must embark on our path. In order for our vision to be clear, we must start walking. Only by being faithful to the light that the Lord gives us at each step of the way can a greater horizon become visible to us. Only by sowing in our life many Advents can we reap the harvest of Christmases.

Weekdays of Advent after December 17

May My Eyes Behold You

"Here he comes…he stands behind our wall" (Ct 2:8-9)
"Elizabeth heard Mary's greeting" (Lk 1:41)

Saint John of the Cross in his Spiritual Canticle says,
> Extinguish these miseries
> Since no one else can stamp them out,
> And my eyes behold you,
> Because you are their light
> And I would open them to you alone.

The holy poet expresses the greatest aspiration of the human being: to see God. It is a wish that becomes more intense as his arrival nears at Christmas.

According to the ancient writers, the sight is the most noble of the senses. The one who sees can know how to keep one's distance; he organizes his field of vision. The one who sees owns already what he looks at; he appropriates it, and he colonizes it. That is why we say he takes it in with his sight. Although Moses did not enter the promised land, he could see it from afar and that was a great consolation. Our sight also often unveils our desire, because it goes ahead, trapping the thing in advance.

There are many ways of seeing. As with the tongue we can do good or evil to our brother, with our sight we have the same power. There are eyes that offend because

December 21

they are laden with impurity and grope whatever they look at. Others, on the other hand, encourage because they are capable of admiring what they see, and so they cheer up. A gaze can have the power to give lots of joy. In the words of Saint John of the Cross, in his Canticle,

> When you looked at me
> Your eyes imprinted your grace in me.

In seeing, there is that which distinguishes persons from the animals. Eagles have very keen eyes that permit them to see their prey in great detail from afar. But only human beings delight in the mere act of seeing. Only for persons is it a delight simply to see. The hunters need to see the prey to reach it and devour it in order to sustain life; while for persons life itself seems to enter through his eyes, because of what he contemplates. One could say like Saint Irenaeus, "The life of man is the vision of God" (Irenaeus, Against Heresies IV:20). And so we learn: there are visions, like the divine one, capable of giving back life to the dead.

What must it be like to see God, the great hope of Christians? What must it be like to allow him to look at us? The first reading gives the feeling that the moment is near. "The voice of my Beloved," the ear reveals that his arrival is near. Elizabeth says the same to Mary in the Gospel, "the moment the sound of your greeting reached my ears, the infant in my womb leaped for joy." The readings still do not speak of the eyes, only of the ears. They are on the edge where Advent, time of listening, will be transformed into Christmas, the time of seeing.

We must train our eyes for the moment in which we will go to the manger and delight in our sight, and when he will give us life as he looks at us.

What must we do, "To see God"? We cannot force God to enter our souls, not even with our eyes: here a possessive look doesn't work. First we need a sight that desires to learn; there are closed gazes that seem to know it all before they even open their eyes. We also need a patient sight. It might seem that the eyes do not require time for learning, that they get the view at the speed of light. Let us remember, however, that Advent is a walk at night, and our pupils need to slowly get used to the darkness. It will be in the night of Bethlehem that God will be born, and we must find him, nearly by feeling, between the ox and the mule.

December 22

To Return Love Back

"I am the woman who stood near you here...I prayed for this child, ...Now I, in turn, give him to the LORD" (1 Sm 1:24-28)
"My soul proclaims the greatness the Lord" (Lk 1:46-56)

We might think, as Christmas approaches, that we have not used this time of Advent as we should. We are in the line with the shepherds. One brings cheese, another a lamb—they all have something to give to the Child. And we may feel that we are coming with empty hands. A Spanish carol says, "I bring him my heart that he may have diapers." But at times it seems that we cannot give even that to Jesus, because our hearts are not prepared for his coming. What should we do? Should we get out of line with the shepherds?

Our readings today give us an answer. Anna, the mother of Samuel, says, "I prayed for this child, and the LORD granted my request. Now *I, in turn, give him to the LORD.*" Mary, on her part, sings the Magnificat in the Gospel, "My soul proclaims the greatness of the Lord." The two mothers are doing the very same thing, because by glorifying God, they are returning his gifts. Our generosity is always leaning on the overflowing generosity we have already received from God.

God, says Saint Irenaeus of Lyon, has not need of our gifts. When he asks us to follow him, it is not because he has need of us following him, but because he wants to give us happiness. In effect, to follow our Savior is to participate in salvation, and to follow the light is to receive the light. "For He is rich, perfect, and in need of nothing. But for this reason does God demand service from people, in order that, since He is good and merciful, He may benefit those who continue in His service. For, as much as God is in want of nothing, so much does man stand in need of fellowship with God. For this is the glory of man, to continue and remain permanently in God's service." (Irenaeus, Against Heresies IV 14:1)

In the carol *Adeste Fideles*, there is a Latin verb, *redamare*, which means to return love for the love received. We can find it in other languages such as Spanish. Maybe it will be helpful to think of this when the road of love seems to be uphill, when you see that your strength is weakening and your heart becomes hardened. In effect, if you do not have the strength to love, maybe you can try something easier: return love for love received. Love as you have been loved and showered with graces, and be grateful.

It does not matter now that time was wasted. Before the stable we will receive new gifts; if our heart has no love, it will be sufficient to look at the Child for it to be filled. If you did not know what to bring the Child on Christmas Eve, pray with Saint Augustine, "Give me

December 22

what you ask for and ask me for whatever you want." The cry of the Child, such a strong symbol of the love of God, will awaken your sleeping heart, "*Sic nos amantem quis non redamaret*? Who would not love Thee, loving us so dearly?"

Weekdays of Advent after December 17

Giving Tomorrow a Name

"He will...turn the hearts of fathers to their children" (Mal 3:24)
"But his mother said in reply: 'No. He will be called John'" (Lk 1:60)

Before the birth of Jesus, the Baptist needed to come, his precursor. Today we hear the story: the child is given birth before the expectation of the whole neighborhood. It is a great surprise to hear the name that the parents are giving him. "He will be called John," says Elizabeth. And Zacharias agrees, writing the name on a tablet before his tongue is freed to sing again the praises of God. "What, then, will this child be?" they all say amazed of what is happening around his birth.

The coming of John the Baptist invites us first to become like children. We have encountered John during all of this Advent: he cried out in the desert; he proclaimed the word; he made paths even. You could feel him also in the end of time, a man of the last days, before the final judgment of God. But it is only now, at the end of the Advent, that we find him as a child. During this Advent journey he has not grown, on the contrary, he is younger as we near Christmas. The path of Advent, we have discovered already, is a path of smallness, a path in which we learn to return to infancy: only the little ones

December 23

will recognize the little one; only the humble can bend down to enter the stable.

Now, before this child, John, we can ask the question that Zachariah and Elisabeth's neighbors ask, "What, then, will this child be?" This question arises whenever a child comes into the world. Every baby brings hope with him and a question about his future. That question arose in our parents when we were born and accompanies us during all our lifetime. What will be my future and my projects?

Before this question, one that should make Elizabeth and Zachariah lose their patience, they give an example of parenthood. They understand that the future of the child is not in their hands. Who can ensure that future of their children will go well—that it will go well even when the parents are no longer present, and that their children will continue to travel the earth? No matter how hard one tries, can one really guarantee that their child will not escape from the paternal home and end his life in disaster?

The parents of the Baptist are not disturbed by these questions, as is demonstrated by the naming of the newborn. A name indicates the mission that the child is called to fulfill during his life; thus it is his future, and it tells what is waiting for him in its future. Elizabeth and Zachariah accept the mission by naming him; they are unafraid of taking such a heavy responsibility. That is because the name has not been given frivolously or because of their expectations, but in accord to God's own designs, "John is his name." Leaning on the Lord, they can offer their son their own shoulders to lean on.

The neighbors are surprised because no one in the family has that name. Prior history—the generations that came before—was not enough to secure the future. There are moments in which new blood is needed to indicate that there are now new paths. All the accumulated experience will not be sufficient to undertake this new challenge. That is why the future of the child can only be guaranteed by the heavenly Father, the owner of tomorrow. As parents, John's parents learned to put their child in better hands, and in that way they are capable to open a horizon for him.

We too, get ready to make ourselves children at the end of this Advent, and to put our own futures in the hands of God and to allow him to name it. Let us not be afraid: the names will not be unfortunate. The ones that the Father confers to us indicate a good star. There are two that he reveals to us during these days of Advent. The first is "John," which indicates the grace and protection of God. The second, "Jesus," meaning God saves.

December 24

Awaken, Oh Man!

"The dawn from on high shall break upon us" (Lk 1:78)

Just before Christmas we realize that the dawn is coming. We sing the antiphon, "Oh, dawn that comes to bring light to man..." We hear in the Gospel the canticle of John's father, the Benedictus: the ancient Zechariah is joyful that the daybreak from on high will visit us to shine on those who sit in darkness and the death's shadow.

When the light calls, there is only one possible response: to awaken. If Advent has prepared us for anything, it is for just that, to not sleep when the sun begins to shine on us. Saint Augustine reminds us in one of his Christmas sermons, "Awaken man, because it is for you that God has become man."

There are many reasons for awakening. Those who are asleep are losing real life. There is a coffee commercial that expresses it well, "Be on guard, life is short." We want to sleep when we are tired, but also when we are courted by sadness or despair.

"Awaken, man, because it is for you that God has become man." That is the fundamental reason for awakening: to remember who we are and our ultimate dignity. Saint Leo the Great will join this chorus, saying on Christmas day, "Recognize, Christian, your dignity."

There is good reason to be awake, to open one's eyes, and not miss life. God has become man for you. You are someone that God has loved so much that he wishes to make himself like you. Your life is worth so much in his eyes, that he cannot bear that it would be lost, and that he has assumed it to himself in order to live it himself, redeeming it from his own time, in joy and in suffering, minute by minute. Human life is so great, that God himself has wished to live it. And by doing so, he has elevated each instant to infinite heights. Awaken, man, because for you God has become man. And there is no dream greater than this reality.

Christmas: Recognizing our Origins

> "And the Word became flesh. /To those who did accept him he gave power to become children of God" (cf. Jn 1:14.12)

The Son of God is born, the son of the Virgin Mary.

Every newborn, when we see him or hold him in our arms, causes us to ask about the mystery of human life. Where has this fragile creature come from? Who has put it into existence? Carlos Murciano has given us a brief dialogue between Joseph and Mary, surprised by the mystery of this birth,

> Tell me, Joseph... or maybe you do not know
> how the hay has become full of living snow,
> here, under the roof?
> Tell me, Joseph, how it is that I have and hold him
> and how went from my womb to the hay
> and returned from the hay to my side.

Here is reflected the surprise of every child that is born and seems in some way, fallen from heaven. All these questions are full of mystery, because each one can direct them to himself. When we were newborns, we also provoked surprise and joy to those who looked at us. We also ask ourselves, where do we come from? From what far off springs comes the river of our history?

The answer to these questions remains obscure to us: no one can remember experiencing his own birth. And yet we urgently need an answer, since the one who has not origins, has not a destiny either. Is our life a product of mere chance? Should we feel thrown into the world, thrown into the midst of a hostile environment? Anyone who has experienced the love of parents in the midst of a family knows that it is not so. For us the world was, from the beginning, a home that embraced us with open arms. And this leads us to realize that life is above all a question of gratitude. From the beginning of our journey there was someone to embrace us and be glad of our existence.

The question, however, is not satisfied purely by the gaze of our parents. They themselves do not know the mystery of our origin. That is what happens to Mary and Joseph, who do not entirely understand the presence of the child in the hay of the stable. All could say as the mother of the Maccabeans, "I do not know how you came to be in my womb; it was not I who gave you breath and life, nor was I who arranged the elements you are made of" (2 Mc 7:22).

So what can we say? If the question has a reply, it must come from a primordial source, prior to the history of the world. Through our parents we must discover the more wise hands that made us and formed us in our mothers' wombs: the hands of God, the Creator. Sometimes however, we do not feel that consoling presence. Is it true that God really cares for us? Isn't he too distant to be occupied with each birth in the world? These are disturbing and fundamental questions in our life.

Then we hear the festive message of Christmas. Here is the Child of Bethlehem come to answer our doubts about the origins of our existence. When we sing to him this Christmas, we confess him to be the eternal son of God, "the Word became flesh (...) and we saw his glory, the glory as of the Father's only Son..." (cf Jn 1:14). We understand that God has an eternal Son, and therefore he is since forever Father. Our God, therefore, is not a solitary God, unaware of everything, isolated in his heavenly world. His life consists of a constant dialogue, a current of love that goes and returns from the Father to the Son.

Even more, today this Son of God, becomes a son of Mary. We could say that the eternal Son, that river of love that comes eternally from the Father, has emptied into the river of human history. From now on, the coming of every child to earth is united with the coming of the beloved Son. Thanks to Christmas, we can say to every child that is born: you do not come from nothing or from chance, but from a love that has begotten you; a love that is born in the very heart of God. So, Alonso de Ledesma's carol hits the target of the Christmas mystery when it sings,

> Sleeping soul, awaken
> and listen to the sweet refrain,
> because this night the Love
> has left a Child at your door.

In effect, the Child that is at the door comes from love. And thanks to him, we can say the same of every child that knocks on life's door. We have been given a son. Now we know that our existence, all that we have and are, comes from the love of God; we know that love is the first spring from which we come and the last horizon of our steps.

Upon arriving at this point, Christmas becomes also a calling. The Child that we contemplate wants us to be born of him, wants us to share his origins from the bosom of the Father. Is that possible? Can a person be born again though old, as Nicodemus asked? When we see our past, we realize that our history weighs us down. If we ask ourselves from whence we come, we could answer: I come from a life of sin, from a history where forgiveness has not happened; I come from injuries that were done to me; I come from offenses and hatreds that do not allow me to look forward...

Today, Christmas day, Jesus tells us that it is possible to recover a pure past, and it is possible to regenerate our history, because it is possible to discover anew the love of the Father in the beginning of everything. Let us remember the tale of the prince that, after being attacked and beaten by some highway men, lost the memory of who he was. Forgotten by all, he roamed his kingdom for many years. However the robbers had left behind one thing: the royal ring of the young man, which was covered with mud. Time passed until the prince noticed the jewel and started to rub it with his clothes to remove the dirt. Then the splendor of the gold shone, and the

Christmas

dignity of the one who wore it was recognized—he was the son of a king. Upon discovering the ring, the prince recovered the memory of his origins and with that, the confidence with which to solve his difficulty. His father, the king, had not stopped looking for him all over the kingdom.

Christmas is the joy of recovering that mark, the royal ring that declares us to be sons of the greatest king, the Creator of the universe. "Recognize, Christian, your dignity," says Saint Leo the Great on this day. Saint Augustine says, "Awaken man, because for you God has become man." And Alonso de Ledesma invited us to awaken, "because this night the Love has left a Child at your door..."

So it is, looking at this Child we can recover our lost dignity, and awaken to the mystery of our origins. It does not matter how much darkness there is in your past. Deeper than the dirty puddles from which the river of life comes, there is a fount of the most pure water, and there is an uncontaminated origin. This water is so plentiful that it rises and purifies all your history, fertilizing your soil and producing much fruit. There is no sin that cannot be pardoned, or scar that cannot be healed.

Awaken, man! Remember your dignity! Before everything, defining from the bud who you are, there is the love of God for you. For you God has become man. And in this manner, the fifth candle of Advent has been lit, the candle of Christmas Eve, "brighter than the noonday..." It is a special light because it does not slip over the surface, but reaches the depth of all existence. There will continue to be darkness in your life, alleys where you cannot find an exit, doubts about what path to take; there will continue to be darkness in your days. But this light will shine in the depths. It will permit you to always see the origin from which you come. It will make clear for you that what you are and what you have take their origin from the love of God for you. By rising above your deepest beginnings, the light of this fifth candle will also open the future. It will inundate the eyes of hope with clarity.

Special Feasts

November 30

St. Andrew: Missionary Advent

"As Jesus was walking by the Sea of Galilee, he saw...Andrew" (Mt 4:18)
"A report goes forth through all the earth" (Ps 18:5)

St. Andrew slips into the Advent, and he does so perfectly in his rights. Because all of his lifetime was full of advents and Christmas, of the hope of the arrival of Jesus, and of the encounter with him...

It's true. Andrew couldn't be present at the stable; he was young when Jesus was born, and his parents were not among the shepherds. His first true Christmas happened by the Jordan, and John tells us it in his Gospel. It is the same chapter in which it is told to us, that "In the beginning was the Word, /and the Word was with God...And the Word became flesh /and made his dwelling among us, /and we saw his glory" (Jn 1:14). Who saw his glory? Right away we hear the story of John and Andrew, disciples of the Baptist, "Rabbi, where are you staying?" And the reply, "Come and you will see."

They saw his glory, the glory of the Word. That glory was fashioned as a call, "come and follow me." It is the Word that became flesh, and it is the Word who calls. And Advent is to get ready to listen to the incarnate Word—that is, the Word who can approach us in any corner of our lives to call us for a concrete following of him.

Since then, St. Andrew will become the messenger of God's advents. He finds immediately afterward Peter, his brother, and he brings him to Jesus (cf. Jn 1:40-41). When some Greeks want to see Jesus, they will come to Philip; Phillip will go and tell to Andrew, and Andrew will be the one to bring them to Jesus (cf Jn 12:22). And it is also his intervention in that miracle of Jesus, when the Teacher multiplied the loaves (cf. Jn 6:8-9). It was Andrew who was the one to point to the boy of that poor offering that would feed the multitude. It is a symbol of our advent: five loaves and two fishes, offered with the hope of a new blessing, to be multiplied in bread for many.

Andrew knew more advents, and the Psalms tells us about them, "The heavens declare the glory of God… /a report goes forth through all the earth." The Church has read since forever this psalm as referred to the preaching of the apostles. "We saw his glory," said St. John. And now that glory is declared and arrives to the ends of the world. Andrew became a town crier of the advents, the bearer of Christmas, of the comings of God to all the earth.

This way, St. Andrew invites us to a missionary advent. The word we await at Christmas is the Word that became flesh, and thus the Word at hand for those who wants to find it. That Word wants to approach you,

November 30

through you. "No one who believes in him will be put to shame," says St. Paul in the first reading. But to show his faithfulness, he needs that you will bring him in your comings and goings through the big city. "How can they believe in him of whom they have not heard?" Today St. Andrew remembers us that every Christian has to be—with his life, words and deeds—a little advent, a prelude of God's coming.

The Immaculate: a Taste of Christmas

> "He chose us in him, before the foundation of the world, to be holy" (Eph 1:4)
> "Hail, full of grace! The Lord is with you" (Lk 1:28)

In the middle of Advent comes the Immaculate. And it does make sense. "I will put enmity between you and the woman, /and between your offspring and hers" (Gn 3:15). It is the proto-gospel, the proto-Christmas, the beforehand announcement that God wants to save humanity.

It started then, after Adam and Eve's fall, a great Advent. God doesn't let the time to go by. He inaugurates at once the age of the hope, before the Bronze Age or the Iron Age. According to St. Irenaeus, after the fall everything was a sign of mercy. God himself took care to find garments to cover the nudity of Adam and Eve; to assure the nourishment for his creatures; and, above all, to promise a saving remedy. Thus Mary, the woman, reminds us of God's great desire for our salvation and his eagerness to turn to each person and find him. So in her the desires of grace came ahead of time.

The Virgin teaches us something more. According to God's desires, his Son should have been born immediately. But the hearts of those who will receive him need to be warmed up; the straw needs to be tidied up, the manger disposed, and the inn asked for hospitality. While the Savior is coming, God sets in the story the presence of a woman. Mary shows the way that it is necessary to prepare carefully to receive the divine gift.

Thus, in Advent there is the presence of Mary. When we see her, we are amazed and full of joy because of the impatience God has to save us, the symbol of his love, of the charity that urges him. At the same time, we listen to his desire that we may cooperate with him, preparing the way and setting the hands of the clock so it may sound at the proper time. The crossing of these two ways will be Christmas, the Son of Mary: Jesus of Nazareth.

The Immaculate calls to our minds another thing. She talks not only about the future, about the coming of God toward us, and the way we may yearn for it. The Immaculate is also the symbol of how we can recover our past. Many times we look backward, and we see the misery of our story—the evil we committed, the wrong we sowed over the earth and that seems to spread boundlessly...Is it possible to regain the peace of the origins?

The Immaculate reminds us today that the way behind us is not closed. God is enough powerful to bring us to the beginning. Despite the sin of Adam and Eve and of every fall that mars the water of history, he makes Mary to come out, Immaculate, in whom shines the cleanness of the original spring. The French writer George Bernanos said about her, "Younger than sin." This way the Virgin becomes the witness of a great hope. What Mary possessed in fullness, conceived without sin, is a sign for us who bear lots of faults on our backs: it is possible to reencounter innocence. The one who discovers in God the primary origin of his existence, has found a deep spring of powerful waters capable of purifying each stratum of his troubled story.

Didaskalos Books

Didaskalos Books is a collection of books written by the Disciples of the Hearts of Jesus and Mary. The "didaskalos" (Gk. "Master") is the one who lights the way and enlarges the horizons of human existence. Beauty comes to our lives through our personal relationships, not through loneliness. The task of the Master is to enhance the richness of human relations and their ability to endure. *Didaskalos Books* exists to make us aware of this magnificent calling: the vocation to love.

Published Titles

1. J. Granados, *The Fifth Candle of Advent*

2. J. Granados and J.A. Granados (eds.), *The Educational Covenant*

Disciples
of the Hearts of
Jesus and Mary

Visit us at www.dcjm.org

Made in the USA
Charleston, SC
12 November 2013